WOMEN OF THE FUR TRADE

SECOND EDITION

FRANCES KONCAN

PLAYWRIGHTS CANADA PRESS

TORONTO

For professional or amateur production rights, please contact:
Colin Rivers, Marquis Literary, 402-10 Adelaide Street East, Toronto, ON M5C 1J3
416-960-9123 X 223 | info@mqlit.ca

LIBRARY AND ARCHIVES CANADA CATALOGUING IN PUBLICATION
Title: Women of the fur trade / Frances Koncan.
Names: Koncan, Frances, author.
Description: Second edition.
Identifiers: Canadiana (print) 20240416740 | Canadiana (ebook) 20240416759
  | ISBN 9780369105158 (softcover) | ISBN 9780369105165 (PDF)
  | ISBN 9780369105172 (EPUB)
Subjects: LCSH: Riel, Louis, 1844-1885—Drama. | LCSH: Métis women—Canada—Drama.
  | LCGFT: Comedy plays. | LCGFT: Drama. | LCGFT: Satirical literature.
Classification: LCC PS8621.O5823 W66 2024 | DDC C812/.6—dc23

Playwrights Canada Press staff work across Turtle Island, on Treaty 7, Treaty 13, and Treaty 20 territories, which are the current and ancestral homes of the Anishinaabe Nations (Ojibwe / Chippewa, Odawa, Potawatomi, Algonquin, Saulteaux, Nipissing, and Mississauga / Michi Saagiig), the Blackfoot Confederacy (Kainai, Piikani, and Siksika), néhiyaw, Sioux, Stoney Nakoda, Tsuut'ina, Wendat, and members of the Haudenosaunee Confederacy (Mohawk, Oneida, Onondaga, Cayuga, Seneca, and Tuscarora), as well as Métis and Inuit peoples. It always was and always will be Indigenous land.

We acknowledge the financial support of the Canada Council for the Arts, the Ontario Arts Council (OAC), Ontario Creates, the Government of Ontario, and the Government of Canada for our publishing activities.

To Louis Riel, the Mr. Brightside of the
Province of Manitoba.

Women of the Fur Trade was first produced by the Royal Manitoba Theatre Centre at the Tom Hendry Warehouse in Winnipeg from February 27 to March 14, 2020, with the following cast and creative team:

Marie-Angelique: Kathleen MacLean
Cecilia: Elizabeth Whitbread
Eugenia: Kelsey Kanatan Wavey
Louis Riel: John Cook
Thomas Scott: Toby Hughes

Director: Audrey Dwyer
Lighting Design: Hugh Conacher
Sound Design: Daniel Roy
Set and Costume Design: Linda Beech
Dramaturg: Lindsay Lachance
Fight Director: Kristen Sawatzky
Apprentice Director: Chelsey Grewar
Stage Manager: Margaret Brook
Apprentice Stage Manager: Zoë Leclerc-Kennedy

SETTING

Eighteen hundred and something something.
A room in a fort on the banks of the Reddish River.

CHARACTERS

Marie-Angelique
Métis Taurus

Cecilia
British Virgo

Eugenia
Ojibwe Sagittarius

Thomas Scott
Irish Capricorn

Louis Riel
Métis Libra

NOTES

All hail the mighty backslash indicating dialogue overlap.
It is very wise, and it looks like this:

/

ONE

We are somewhere. It's dark.

There are three rocking chairs and not much else.

There are, however, walls, which are covered in portraits of men: famous men, infamous men, nobody men, somebody men, men without hats, men with brooms, men who sold the world, men who fell to Earth, Men of the Fur Trade, men of all kinds, men all over the place—just like in real life.

There is also a floor, as is often the case in places like these. It's an odd sort of floor.

Three women sit in their rocking chairs.

They wear fur coats.

They have recently woken up and are playing a game.

MARIE-ANGELIQUE: "In the future, everyone will be famous for fifteen minutes."

CECILIA: Andy Warhol. "Certain shades of limelight wreck a girl's complexion."

MARIE-ANGELIQUE: Truman Capote, *Breakfast at Tiffany's*. "Upon this a question arises: Whether it be better to be loved than feared or feared than loved?"

CECILIA: Niccolò di Bernardo dei Machiavelli!

MARIE-ANGELIQUE: Yes! Ugh hot.

CECILIA: "A hero is no braver than an ordinary man, but he is brave five minutes longer."

MARIE-ANGELIQUE: *(to EUGENIA)* Hey. Are you going to play this time or not?

EUGENIA: I don't like games.

MARIE-ANGELIQUE: Remember what happened last time . . .

EUGENIA: . . . Fine. Ralph Waldo Emerson.

CECILIA: Yay! Fun!

EUGENIA: "I have never in my life yelled at a girl like this. I was rooting for you. We were all rooting for you. How dare you."

MARIE-ANGELIQUE: Tyra Banks, *America's Next Top Model* cycle four.

CECILIA: Penalty. Against the rules.

EUGENIA: Why?

CECILIA: We can't quote women. That doesn't count.

MARIE-ANGELIQUE: She wasn't quoting women; she was quoting Tyra.

CECILIA: Still. It's wrong. You forfeit your turn, and now it's mine. "All who have their reward on earth, the fruits of painful superstition and blind zeal, naught seeking but the praise of men, here find fit retribution, empty as their deed."

MARIE-ANGELIQUE: John Milton, *Paradise Lost*. I said it first. Shut up. You shut up!

EUGENIA: *Paradise Lost*, John Milton. I said it first. Shut up. You shut up!

MARIE-ANGELIQUE: "Are we human or are we dancer?"

CECILIA: Improper grammar—

EUGENIA: Didn't write it.

MARIE-ANGELIQUE: Brandon Flowers, heterosexual lead singer of my favourite band, the Killers, and the world's second favourite Mormon after Donny Osmond.

CECILIA: My second favourite Mormon is the man from *Angels in / America*—

MARIE-ANGELIQUE: Nobody asked you who your second favourite Mormon / was—

CECILIA: Nobody ever asks me anything! I don't want to play this game anymore. Would anyone care for some tea?

MARIE-ANGELIQUE: "I know that through the grace of God, I am the founder of Manitoba."

CECILIA: Louis Riel. "We must cherish our inheritance. We must preserve our nationality for the youth of our future. The story should be written down to pass on."

MARIE-ANGELIQUE: Louis Riel. "I have nothing but my heart and I have given it long ago to my country."

EUGENIA: Louis Riel. "In a little while it will be over. We may fail. But the rights for which we contend will not die."

MARIE-ANGELIQUE: Louis Riel. "My people will sleep for one hundred years, but when they awake, it will be the artists who give them their spirit back."

The fort lurches like a great beast waking from hibernation.

But it's only a false alarm.

CECILIA: Well I'm gonna have some tea so—

MARIE-ANGELIQUE: I'm bored—

EUGENIA: New game?

MARIE-ANGELIQUE: New game!

EUGENIA: New game! What kind?

MARIE-ANGELIQUE: I don't know. Wait, I know. David Attenborough Documentary!

CECILIA: That's not fair, you know how much I love men telling me about things I don't care about.

MARIE-ANGELIQUE: Then play.

CECILIA: I'm DRINKING my TEA.

A new game begins.

EUGENIA: The year is—

MARIE-ANGELIQUE: Eighteen hundred and something something!

EUGENIA: And the place is—

CECILIA: A fort!

EUGENIA: Somewhere upon the banks of a Reddish River, in—

ALL: Treaty One!

They say this the way people at a Winnipeg Jets game shout "true north" during the national anthem.

EUGENIA: —territory, nearish or uponish what is now known as Winnipeg, Manitoba, Canada—

CECILIA: Lovely place!

EUGENIA: —a city known for simultaneously being the Murder Capital of Canada and the Most Racist City in Canada.

CECILIA: We're also the Slurpee Capital of Canada. Don't forget that. That's very important. It should be a part of the treaty, don't you think?

MARIE-ANGELIQUE: Honestly, I don't even know what a treaty is. I just / pretend like I do so nobody judges me.

CECILIA: Hard same.

EUGENIA: A treaty is an agreement / between—

CECILIA: We must ask the men! The men will know.

CECILIA approaches the portrait of THOMAS SCOTT.

Meet Thomas Scott. Irish. Protestant. Dreamy and delightful. Despite his advanced age of twenty-eight years, he retains many of the assets of his youthful prime, such as silky, smooth, pale alabaster skin that you want to lick as if it's a glazed ham, and luscious long legs that resemble a gazelle. They seem endless, both in terms of length and in terms of possibilities. Although not traditionally handsome, his banging beach bod is so kickin' it makes you forget all about the butterface. And he always parts his light brown hair slightly to the left. I myself am married, but if I wasn't . . .

CECILIA holds up a doll version of THOMAS SCOTT.

(as THOMAS SCOTT) A treaty is an agreement. And I, for one, would like to honour all of our . . . agreements . . . and humbly acknowledge the traditional lands upon which we stand, and offer a knowledge exchange, a prayer of my people. Treaty, treaty, reconciliation. Treaty, treaty, God bless this nation. Treaty, treaty in a boat, treaty, treaty with a goat. Amen.

MARIE-ANGELIQUE applauds enthusiastically and gives a standing ovation.

MARIE-ANGELIQUE: *Bravo! Fantastique! Très bien! Encore!*

MARIE-ANGELIQUE runs to the LOUIS RIEL portrait.

Louis Riel!!! Métis, like me. Hot, but doesn't even know it. Like, model-level. Despite being hot, he is also smart, which is so rare, y'know? His focus on his work has led him to neglect his appearance, so he's kind of undernourished in that tortured artist way . . . he's a bit dishevelled, and you really have to peer through the layers to see the true beauty within his heart. Also, I think he wears glasses? Because he's a bit of a nerd, which is good! Or else he would be totally unrelatable and intimidating to women. Louis Riel.

CECILIA holds up her THOMAS SCOTT doll.

CECILIA: *(as THOMAS SCOTT)* Louis Riel.

MARIE-ANGELIQUE pulls out a LOUIS RIEL doll.

A different game.

Maybe a game within a game.

MARIE-ANGELIQUE: *(as LOUIS RIEL)* Thomas Scott.

CECILIA: *(as THOMAS SCOTT)* Big Lou.

MARIE-ANGELIQUE: *(as LOUIS RIEL)* Tiny Tom.

CECILIA: *(as THOMAS SCOTT)* How did you find me here?

MARIE-ANGELIQUE: *(as LOUIS RIEL)* Instagram.

CECILIA: *(as THOMAS SCOTT)* I specifically asked them not to tag me.

MARIE-ANGELIQUE: *(as LOUIS RIEL)* It hurts, doesn't it? When you are betrayed by the people you trust the most . . . the people you thought were your friends.

CECILIA: *(as THOMAS SCOTT)* What are you implying?

MARIE-ANGELIQUE: *(as LOUIS RIEL)* I'm not implying anything. I'm directly saying that I know you have aligned with the enemy in order to steal our land, and I refuse to let that happen!

CECILIA: *(as THOMAS SCOTT)* Oh, pish posh. You'll never win, Louis. Or should I call you Lewis?

MARIE-ANGELIQUE: *(as LOUIS RIEL)* Don't, man. You know I hate that.

CECILIA: *(as THOMAS SCOTT)* The land will be ours eventually, whether you half-breeds and savages hand it over to us or we take it by force.

MARIE-ANGELIQUE: *(as LOUIS RIEL)* We will never give this land to you!!!

CECILIA: *(as THOMAS SCOTT)* It is unstoppable. It is manifest destiny.

MARIE-ANGELIQUE: *(as LOUIS RIEL)* Your mom manifested my destiny last night.

CECILIA: *(as THOMAS SCOTT)* Wow. Well. I guess this is it. Guess this is war.

MARIE-ANGELIQUE: *(as LOUIS RIEL)* Looks like it.

CECILIA: *(as THOMAS SCOTT)* I'm unfollowing you.

MARIE-ANGELIQUE: *(as LOUIS RIEL)* Like I care.

CECILIA: *(as THOMAS SCOTT)* I'm leaving.

MARIE-ANGELIQUE: *(as LOUIS RIEL)* No, I'm leaving.

CECILIA: *(as THOMAS SCOTT)* I'm leaving first.

MARIE-ANGELIQUE: *(as LOUIS RIEL)* I'm already gone.

CECILIA: *(as THOMAS SCOTT)* I was never even here.

MARIE-ANGELIQUE: *(as LOUIS RIEL)* I'm an astral projection.

CECILIA: *(as THOMAS SCOTT)* I'm a hologram.

MARIE-ANGELIQUE: *(as LOUIS RIEL)* *Au revoir*, sir.

CECILIA: *(as THOMAS SCOTT)* See you on the battlefield.

MARIE-ANGELIQUE: *(as LOUIS RIEL)* Maybe I'll see you there or maybe I'll see you somewhere else.

CECILIA: . . . Uh, sorry, is he coming to the battlefield or what?

MARIE-ANGELIQUE: Oh yeah yeah, for sure, he'll totally be there.

EUGENIA: Aren't we a little too old to play with dolls?

MARIE-ANGELIQUE and CECILIA get serious.

Now, where were we?

MARIE-ANGELIQUE: The fort.

EUGENIA: Ah, yes. The fort. The fort in which we live is a totally normal fort with nothing suspicious happening.

CECILIA: It is a fort much like Lower Fort Garry or Upper Fort Garry, but it is not either of the actual Fort Garries.

MARIE-ANGELIQUE: It has never even heard of anybody named Garry. And who are we? We are the Women of the Fur Trade. You probably haven't heard of us. That's okay: we probably haven't heard of you either.

A triangle dings.

EUGENIA: Well, that's me. I must go.

CECILIA: Again?

EUGENIA: Yes, again. Now, have fun, be safe, don't sit in my chair, and I'll catch you two on the flippity flip.

EUGENIA boogies off into the night, blowing a kiss to the portrait of Gabriel Dumont on her way out.

TWO

MARIE-ANGELIQUE stands up and sits in EUGENIA's chair: another game begins, one that continues in perpetuity.

MARIE-ANGELIQUE and CECILIA rock back and forth and back and forth and back and forth in the rocking chairs, in perfect unison, caressing their dolls.

MARIE-ANGELIQUE: I hear he's tall. Taller than me. Six foot three, easy peasy. Like Castro.

CECILIA: I hear he's buff. Huge muscles. Benches four hundred, never breaks a sweat.

MARIE-ANGELIQUE: He's an inspiring leader. Charismatic. Great at speeches.

CECILIA: He's confident and masculine and doesn't need anyone's approval for anything.

MARIE-ANGELIQUE: So brave, so courageous, always ready for battle.

CECILIA: So smart. So wise. He has seen the world and knows all its secrets.

MARIE-ANGELIQUE: Decisive. Definitive.

CECILIA: Pious. Devout.

MARIE-ANGELIQUE: He never, ever yells.

CECILIA: And he's greatly esteemed by all who encounter him.

MARIE-ANGELIQUE: Truly, a hero.

CECILIA: A hero, truly.

They swoon like fictional characters in a Harlequin romance novel.

MARIE-ANGELIQUE: Do you really believe in manifest destiny?

CECILIA: What? No, no, no, no nono, I was simply being . . . Thomas Scott. Presumably he does. My husband sure does.

MARIE-ANGELIQUE: Ew.

CECILIA: I know. But you have nothing to worry about. You fit in here so well, sitting and rocking and smiling.

MARIE-ANGELIQUE smiles.

MARIE-ANGELIQUE: I wish I could meet him. He's so hot. I feel such a . . . kinship.

CECILIA: I don't think kinship is the word for that feeling, but okay.

MARIE-ANGELIQUE: I feel like I'm on fire inside.

CECILIA: Yeah, not kinship.

MARIE-ANGELIQUE: Eugenia is so lucky. She gets to leave whenever she wants. She gets to go anywhere and do anything. She could be with Louis Riel right now. They could be having—

CECILIA: Kinship?

MARIE-ANGELIQUE: Do not mock me, Cecilia. There is a reckoning coming and I intend to reckon with it, somehow. For I believe in Louis Riel, and I believe in his great cause, and I believe in a thing called love, and I believe that there is more to life than sitting and rocking and drinking tea. And if I've learned anything useful from my mother at all, which is unlikely, it would be this: if you can believe it, you can achieve it.

CECILIA: How *is* your mother?

MARIE-ANGELIQUE: Let's not ruin a beautiful day by thinking of horrible things.

CECILIA coughs.

Are you okay?

CECILIA: A tickle in my throat. Absolutely nothing serious or relevant to the plot.

MARIE-ANGELIQUE: K. Ugh. I'm so bored here. Free me, Louis. I'm your number one fan!

CECILIA: My husband met him once. Did not think very highly of him.

MARIE-ANGELIQUE: Yes, but his opinion cannot be trusted. After all, your husband is friends with John A. Macdonald, prime minister of Canada and the most tiresome and least hot man on the planet.

CECILIA: I actually find Sir John to be rather alluring in a sickly / sort of way—

MARIE-ANGELIQUE stops rocking in her chair and gasps.

MARIE-ANGELIQUE: Ooh. Your husband! Of course! Of course. PERHAPS. Perhaps you could speak to him on my behalf. Perhaps something could be arranged. A spontaneous, unplanned meeting? An accidental encounter? You are my oldest and dearest and only friend, and I admire you most ardently, and would be loyal to you forever in exchange for this one small favour.

CECILIA: I am happy to try, of course, for you and for our eternal, unbreakable, very stable friendship. But I doubt he'll help. All he cares about is land.

MARIE-ANGELIQUE: This is about the land!

CECILIA: And crops.

MARIE-ANGELIQUE: Crops grow on land!

CECILIA: And sons.

> CECILIA *rubs her stomach. I should have mentioned this before, but she is visibly pregnant.*

It's been girls, girls, girls all up in here.

MARIE-ANGELIQUE: I do hope for your husband's sake that your next baby is a boy. What will you name it?

CECILIA: Victoria, if it is a girl, after the queen, of course. If it's a boy, I was thinking maybe . . . Thomas, after . . . after . . .

> CECILIA *gazes adoringly at her* THOMAS SCOTT.

MARIE-ANGELIQUE: Touch grass.

CECILIA: Yeah, I know, but he's just so cute.

MARIE-ANGELIQUE: He's a member of the Canadian Party, and an Orangeman, *and* a Protestant. That's three very not cool things.

CECILIA: I think that depends on who you ask.

MARIE-ANGELIQUE: He wants to take our land and kill us all!

CECILIA: Not *me*, *I'm* white.

MARIE-ANGELIQUE: Sometimes I don't know whose side you're on.

CECILIA: I'm not on anybody's side. I'm just trying to survive. As are we all. But no matter what happens in the future, I promise I would never betray you, Marie-Angelique. Cross my heart and hope to die. Pinky swear.

MARIE-ANGELIQUE: . . . Pinky swear. Friends forever. No man, no land, and no government shall ever come between us. We'll always have each other's backs.

They pinky swear.

EUGENIA re-enters with a handbag full of furs.

EUGENIA: Yo. Got furs.

CECILIA: Eugenia!

MARIE-ANGELIQUE: What are you doing back so soon?

CECILIA: I'll put the kettle on.

EUGENIA: The seasons have been shorter lately. And I'm very efficient. Why are you in my chair? I told you not to sit in my chair.

MARIE-ANGELIQUE stands up and moves back to her original rocking chair. EUGENIA sits down in her rightful traditional spot.

CECILIA: Welcome back, my dear friend.

MARIE-ANGELIQUE: Any news? Will there be a rebellion? I've always wanted to be part of a rebellion.

The sound of a boiling teapot.

EUGENIA: It is imminent.

MARIE-ANGELIQUE: I knew it! I knew Confederation was a dumb-ass idea.

CECILIA: Hopefully the battle will not reach us. I will pray for peace and our safety. Our father, who art in heaven, hallowed be thy—

The tea is ready.

Tea! The tea is ready. It's time for tea! Shall we have some tea? Tee hee.

CECILIA gives each of the women a teacup, a saucer, and a spoon.

MARIE-ANGELIQUE: *Merci.*

CECILIA: *La bibliothèque.*

EUGENIA: *Miigwetch.*

CECILIA: Oooh and a very May-witch to you too!

The three women raise their teacups and have a silent toast. MARIE-ANGELIQUE and CECILIA each take a sip. It's apparently delish.

Yum.

EUGENIA turns her teacup over. Nothing drips out.

EUGENIA: There's nothing in this / cup—

CECILIA: Eugenia, where do you go when you leave us behind?

EUGENIA: All over. Wherever I want.

CECILIA: Isn't it dangerous?

EUGENIA: Of course. But it's dangerous here too.

EUGENIA motions to the men.

MARIE-ANGELIQUE: I kind of like them. I like being watched.

EUGENIA: I bet they'd love to watch you even more if you were wearing, say, a new fur hat?

EUGENIA pulls out a fur hat.

MARIE-ANGELIQUE: Oh, it's beautiful! But I have nothing to trade! And I have none of that new-fangled Confederate currency because I don't have a new-fangled Confederate husband. God, my life sucks.

EUGENIA: Cecilia?

CECILIA: My husband will no longer trade with women. He says it's against the Lord's will. Says it is not natural for women to be off in the world, working alongside men.

EUGENIA: Weird. Where I come from, women were always responsible for trading. You can't trust men with important jobs. Best just send them off to like fishing or a war, somewhere they won't be in the way, and bring them back when you need them, if you know what I mean. But, quite frankly, in my opinion, there's almost nothing a man can do that a woman can't do . . . again, if you know what I mean. And I know you do, Cecilia.

CECILIA: I most certainly do not!

MARIE-ANGELIQUE: What do you mean?

CECILIA: You'll find out when you're married.

MARIE-ANGELIQUE: Do you mean sexual intercourse?

CECILIA: It is not appropriate for women to speak of such things.

EUGENIA: Where I'm from, women always—

CECILIA: We are no longer where you're from. That world is gone.

EUGENIA: A final gasp. A dying breath. A good fur trade.

MARIE-ANGELIQUE: It is not dead yet. Our way of life can still be saved. And we can all still be friends and trade furs forever! Furever! Haha! Trust me. Louis Riel will see to it.

EUGENIA: Ugh.

MARIE-ANGELIQUE: May I help you?

EUGENIA: Everywhere I go that's all I hear. Louis Riel this, Louis Riel that. He's overrated.

MARIE-ANGELIQUE: Blasphemer.

CECILIA: I've heard he is very pious and devout, although there are murmurs that he may be a . . . whisper voice traitor end whisper voice.

MARIE-ANGELIQUE: Even a traitor deserves forgiveness.

EUGENIA: His face looks like a potato.

MARIE-ANGELIQUE: Potatoes are delicious. I'm sure Thomas Scott would agree.

CECILIA: Why? Because he's Irish? / That's kinda raci—

EUGENIA: And what's with his facial hair these days? A mustache with no beard?

MARIE-ANGELIQUE: He's a trendsetter.

CECILIA: Your mother would never approve.

MARIE-ANGELIQUE: My mother is a selfish, miserable hag and I'll never forgive her.

EUGENIA: Have you tried therapy?

CECILIA: Didn't you just say that "even a traitor deserves forgiveness"?

MARIE-ANGELIQUE: We digress from the important matter at hand: the newly formed country of Canada is intent on destroying our way of life and I must use all of my skills and all of my gumption to survive! I am like the Scarlett O'Hara of the prairies, and I will do whatever it takes to protect my people. And I will also go on record to say that it has always been my childhood dream to marry a Métis man and keep our culture alive.

CECILIA: No, it wasn't. You've always loved basic white boys.

MARIE-ANGELIQUE: They're just so confident, for no good reason!

EUGENIA: Do we even know for sure if he is Métis? He could be faking it. People do that all the time, for book deals.

CECILIA: I believe he is Ojibwe, Eugenia. Like you.

EUGENIA: He's *Franco*-Ojibwe. That's completely different.

CECILIA: How is it different?

EUGENIA: Well, for one, I don't *parle pas français*.

MARIE-ANGELIQUE: You do too *parle pas français*. We all *parle pas français*.

EUGENIA: Mine's *no bueno*.

MARIE-ANGELIQUE: It is no longer fashionable to look down upon the French, Eugenia. It is *très* chic now. The Russians, for instance, can't get enough of it.

CECILIA: TOLSTOY.

MARIE-ANGELIQUE: Exactly.

EUGENIA: But why marriage? That's not fun.

CECILIA: I'm having a great time.

MARIE-ANGELIQUE: Because I'm not like you, Eugenia. I can't just leave here whenever I want. I can't trap or hunt or take care of myself. If I get married, I'll be protected. Right, Cecilia?

CECILIA: Right!

MARIE-ANGELIQUE: And if I'm protected, then I'll have more power to protect and help others. Right, Cecilia?

CECILIA: Oh, I haven't really thought / about it.

EUGENIA: That's sort of noble in a selfish sort of way.

MARIE-ANGELIQUE: Exactly! That's how history will remember me. Selfish, noble, and extremely well-dressed.

EUGENIA: History won't remember us, Marie-Angelique. History is written by the victors. And the victors are always men.

CECILIA: Amen!

MARIE-ANGELIQUE: Then I'll just have to write my own history.

CECILIA: Oh, gosh.

EUGENIA: . . . That could be fun.

MARIE-ANGELIQUE: Right? So this is what I'm thinking: Louis Riel is surely at the forefront of the fight for our rights, and that fight will inevitably bring him here. And when it does, I'll be ready.

CECILIA: Ready for what?

MARIE-ANGELIQUE: For whatever it takes! If I must wed, then wed I shall. If I must fight, then I shall fight. And if I must be hanged for my actions, then gather the audience and string up that noose, baby, because this neck is ready to be choked to death.

CECILIA: Jesus Christ.

MARIE-ANGELIQUE: But a wedding would be best.

EUGENIA: You don't even know him.

MARIE-ANGELIQUE: Well, that's about to change, because Cecilia's husband is going to introduce us.

CECILIA: I mean, I said I'd ask him.

EUGENIA: Even if you did meet him, there's no telling you'd like him.

MARIE-ANGELIQUE: You don't have to like someone to marry them, Eugenia.

CECILIA: Truly. With such high standards, it's no wonder you're not married yet.

EUGENIA: I don't intend to ever get married.

CECILIA gasps.

I like being free.

MARIE-ANGELIQUE: I can be free and be a wife at the same time.

CECILIA: No. You must submit to your husband fully. Every decision he makes, you must support.

MARIE-ANGELIQUE: Oh. Okay. So I'll simply . . . pray that he makes good choices.

CECILIA: Yes, we must all pray, all the time, every day.

EUGENIA: Last I heard, he had dropped out of school and was living in Chicago writing, like, poetry.

MARIE-ANGELIQUE: Chicago? Is that far from here?

EUGENIA: Yes.

MARIE-ANGELIQUE: Maybe I could go to Chicago.

CECILIA: What? Leave the fort?

EUGENIA: You haven't left the fort for years.

MARIE-ANGELIQUE: I haven't wanted to. But how can I just sit here and wait / when there's—

CECILIA: Sometimes sitting and waiting is the most womanly thing a person can do.

MARIE-ANGELIQUE: You're right, Cecilia. If it is meant to be, it will be. If it is meant to be, he will come and find me. For distance is no barrier. Love knows no obstacles. And as long as we have love, love will keep us together.

> *A letter magically drops from the ceiling and into CECILIA's lap. She picks it up and reads it.*

CECILIA: Prithee, hark. I have just received a letter from my husband. He will be returning to Reddish River shortly, alongside his expedition, on the trail of a certain . . . ooh, Marie-Angelique, you will find this news of particular interest . . . Mister Louis Riel.

MARIE-ANGELIQUE: Oh my god.

EUGENIA: The trail of who?

MARIE-ANGELIQUE: Oh my god.

CECILIA: Louis Riel.

> *EUGENIA begins rocking in her chair. She rocks back and forth and back and forth and back and forth.*

MARIE-ANGELIQUE: Oh my god, it's all happening. This is happening. This is really happening. I honestly thought I was being a little unreasonable, but this is . . . all my dreams are coming true! Everything I've worked so hard for! Every croissant I never ate, every Pilates class I ever attended, every time I told my former crush, Matthew the Incompetent Blacksmith, "No, I'm saving myself for Louis Riel"—it was all worth it. Because I was. I truly was.

EUGENIA: Matthew the Incompetent Blacksmith is a good, kind man. He's a wise match and he looks great shirtless and can make dope swords.

MARIE-ANGELIQUE: But I love another!

EUGENIA: No, you don't. You've never even met him.

MARIE-ANGELIQUE: So what? None of us have.

EUGENIA stops rocking.

MARIE-ANGELIQUE: No.	CECILIA: No way.
Wait what?	Huh?
Have you?	You have?
Oh my god.	Oh, my lanta.
You've met Louis Riel?	You've met Louis Riel!

MARIE-ANGELIQUE and CECILIA shriek with excitement and maybe a little bit of jealousy.

MARIE-ANGELIQUE: My future husband is coming home and my dearest, bestest, and onlyest friend will introduce us! Oh, this is perfect! Perfect, perfect, perfect!

MARIE-ANGELIQUE warmly embraces EUGENIA. CECILIA gasps.

EUGENIA: I always got the feeling you didn't like me very much.

MARIE-ANGELIQUE: Nonsense! You are my best friend forever—

CECILIA: Hey, what about ME?

MARIE-ANGELIQUE: —and *you* will introduce me to Louis Riel!

CECILIA: I thought I was your best friend.

MARIE-ANGELIQUE: Best friend is a tier, not a person.

EUGENIA: He's so mediocre.

MARIE-ANGELIQUE: He is not mediocre. He is a man. He matters.

CECILIA: How well *do* you know him, Eugenia?

EUGENIA: Surely it would be improper to discuss such things.

MARIE-ANGELIQUE: . . . Liar.

CECILIA: Scandalous.

MARIE-ANGELIQUE: He would never. He's too good for you. But you will introduce me, won't you?

EUGENIA: I don't know if that's a good idea.

MARIE-ANGELIQUE: I'll buy one of your hats.

EUGENIA: I thought you didn't have any money.

MARIE-ANGELIQUE takes off her necklace.

MARIE-ANGELIQUE: Here. A trade. It was my mother's, she made it herself.

EUGENIA: It's beautiful. But I can't take this. This is worth more than just one fur hat.

MARIE-ANGELIQUE: So bring me another, and another, until we're even. Come on, take it. If you don't sell these hats your family will starve, won't they? So take it. It's valuable and it doesn't mean anything to me. Anymore.

They trade.

CECILIA: Oh, Marie-Angelique, your lifelong dream is about to come true.

MARIE-ANGELIQUE: Yes, it is. For soon I shall be on my way to becoming Mrs. Louis Riel!

And with a grand flourish, she puts on her fluffy new hat.

THREE

The women each grab a piece of paper and a quill—but no ink—from their bags, and each begin to compose a letter.

CECILIA: Dear Husband,

EUGENIA: Dear Prime Minister,

MARIE-ANGELIQUE: Dear Louis,

EUGENIA: How dare you.

CECILIA: Your child was born, a sweet little girl.

MARIE-ANGELIQUE: You don't know me, and we've never met, but I am writing to you now to profess my undying love.

EUGENIA: I hate you.

CECILIA: Curly, blond hair with fair skin.

MARIE-ANGELIQUE: Forgive me if that's forward, but I am a very direct person and I am confident you will find my assertiveness charming, for you have such wonderful taste in all areas of your life.

EUGENIA: It's time to make way, for the times are changing.

CECILIA: Very Aryan.

MARIE-ANGELIQUE: I would like to be so bold as to propose a meeting between the two of us, upon your return to the Reddish River.

CECILIA: I miss you.

EUGENIA: Our turtle's back has been burdened by your boringness for far too long.

CECILIA: I can't live without you by my side.

MARIE-ANGELIQUE: Our mutual friend, dear sweet Eugenia, believes we will get along swimmingly, and I agree.

CECILIA: You are so honourable to fight for our safety, but I really think a job closer to home would be best for our growing family.

EUGENIA: You need to watch how a real leader leads and change your plans.

MARIE-ANGELIQUE: Oh yes, my name is Marie-Angelique.

CECILIA: Your children love you and so do I.

EUGENIA: The world is rearranging, it's marching onward, and time moves on without those who refuse to evolve.

CECILIA: We pray for your safe return every night.

MARIE-ANGELIQUE: I am twenty-two years old, and a Taurus with Sun rising in Leo, so I hate change, and as you are a Libra on the cusp of Scorpio, I envision a thrilling meeting of the minds is fated for us.

CECILIA: And Thomas Scott too, I hope that he's all right.

EUGENIA: Revolution is in the air.

MARIE-ANGELIQUE: I eagerly await your arrival to our beautiful fort. I can't wait to meet you and hope I may be able to contribute meaningfully to your noble cause.

EUGENIA: You'll be lost and left behind, and I will celebrate with Prosecco and strawberries.

CECILIA: He is a lovely man, with an excellent side part, and is an asset to our chance for survival.

MARIE-ANGELIQUE: Some people may call you selfish, but I value your devoted leadership.

EUGENIA: "You may take our land, you may take our lives, but you will never take our freedom." ·

CECILIA: I hope we can withstand the transformation.

EUGENIA: Mel Gibson, *Braveheart.*

MARIE-ANGELIQUE: You are a Métis man of esteem and prestige.

CECILIA: I must admit I have some hesitation.

MARIE-ANGELIQUE: And I am a Métis woman of . . . well, let's just say, you could do worse.

EUGENIA: If you hurt Gabriel Dumont, I will end you.

CECILIA: But I pray each day for a better nation.

MARIE-ANGELIQUE: Goodbye for now, and safe travels.

CECILIA: Your obedient wife,

EUGENIA: Fuck off and die,

MARIE-ANGELIQUE: Lots of love,

CECILIA: Cecilia.

EUGENIA: Your mom.

MARIE-ANGELIQUE: Marie-Angelique. Xoxo.

EUGENIA and MARIE-ANGELIQUE seal up their letters.

CECILIA: P.S. Do hurry back. The conflict marches ever closer, and I fear for my safety and the safety of our children.

CECILIA seals up her letter. She has a slight coughing fit. The three women throw their letters high in the air, where they are picked up by Canada Post and delivered in a timely and efficient manner.

FOUR

Meanwhile, deep inside the portraits and far beyond the walls of the Not-Fort-Garry Fort Garry sit THOMAS SCOTT *and* LOUIS RIEL *in two non-rocking chairs. They do not wear furs. They do not drink tea. They do not look anything like their portraits.*

LOUIS dictates the end of a letter to THOMAS.

LOUIS RIEL: . . . and in conclusion, mark my words, the prairies will be alive once more with the sound of music, the sound of drums, the sound of war. The sanguine fluid of our enemies, our friends, and ourselves will circumvolute and transmogrify the waters of the Reddish River and turn it into a river of blood and a tributary of forsaken dreams. Have a great day, your friend, Louis Riel.

THOMAS SCOTT: That's nice. Very poetic.

LOUIS RIEL: It's not nice.

THOMAS SCOTT: Okay.

LOUIS RIEL: Nice is a cowardly word, Thomas.

THOMAS SCOTT: Okay.

LOUIS RIEL: Do better next time.

THOMAS SCOTT: Okay.

THOMAS finishes the letter and throws it up for express delivery.

Done.

LOUIS is silent.

You're welcome.

LOUIS RIEL: Hm? Oh. Thanks, man.

THOMAS smiles. He's a little starved for gratitude. His confidence has risen enormously.

THOMAS SCOTT: You're welcome . . . Hey, man?

LOUIS RIEL: Yeah, man?

THOMAS SCOTT: Can we talk? Like man to man?

LOUIS RIEL: Bro to bro?

THOMAS SCOTT: Yeah.

LOUIS RIEL: Cool dude to cool dude.

THOMAS SCOTT: Okay sure.

LOUIS RIEL: Then okay sure to you too also as well.

THOMAS SCOTT: Right. Um, so I love, first of all, writing all your letters for you. I really do. I'm honoured. It's just the best how you get so many letters and I don't get any, so it's great, it's . . . so good . . . just . . . writing things . . . for you, and not for me, but uh . . . like I'm glad my hands are keeping busy or else, you know, who knows what else I'd be doing with them, haha that was a joke, you didn't get it, sorry. Look, Louis, I know we've had our differences, but . . . sorry, I don't know exactly how to say this, I—

LOUIS RIEL: Say it like a man, Thomas.

THOMAS SCOTT: I . . . okay. I sometimes feel like, like, like, like you—

LOUIS RIEL: A real man never stutters.

THOMAS SCOTT: Sorry.

LOUIS RIEL: Start again. Use your words.

THOMAS clears his throat.

THOMAS SCOTT: Sometimes. I feel. Like you. Don't respect. Me.

LOUIS RIEL: And?

THOMAS SCOTT: That was it. That's all.

LOUIS RIEL: Hm.

THOMAS SCOTT: Well, do . . . do you?

LOUIS RIEL: Do I what?

THOMAS SCOTT: Respect me?

LOUIS RIEL: Does the grey wolf respect the Connemara pony?

THOMAS SCOTT: I beg your pardon?

LOUIS RIEL: You heard me.

THOMAS SCOTT: I heard you, but I didn't hear you. I'm going to need additional context.

LOUIS RIEL: I'm a grey wolf, a highly revered and feared animal here on the prairies, and you are a mere Irish pony, the natural prey of wolves like me. See, you're not even a horse, Thomas, you're a pony.

That's a tiny horse.

THOMAS SCOTT: I know what a pony is.

LOUIS RIEL: Good.

THOMAS SCOTT: But you should know that wolves went extinct in Ireland over a hundred years ago.

LOUIS RIEL: You're not in Ireland anymore, old sport. This is Canada: a much more dangerous place, for all of us, wolves and ponies alike.

Suddenly, a letter falls from the sky and into LOUIS's lap. He inspects it. It has a bright lipstick mark on it.

Ugh, not another one.

LOUIS fans himself lackadaisically.

THOMAS SCOTT: Ooh! Are you going to read it?

LOUIS RIEL: There's a war going on, Thomas. I don't have time for fan letters.

THOMAS SCOTT: I wish I'd get a fan letter.

LOUIS RIEL: Then here. Take it?

THOMAS SCOTT: Really?

LOUIS RIEL: Sure. It's all yours. Knock yourself out.

LOUIS hands THOMAS the letter. THOMAS opens it and begins to read.

THOMAS SCOTT: "Dear Louis,

You don't know me, and we've never met, but I am writing to you now to profess my undying love." Wow. That's bold, I like it.

LOUIS RIEL: I meant read it silently to yourself.

THOMAS SCOTT: Okay, sorry.

LOUIS RIEL: Well now I'm invested, so keep reading aloud.

THOMAS SCOTT: Okay. "I would like to be so bold—" see, BOLD "—as to propose a meeting between the two of us, upon your return to the Reddish River." Reddish River? Is that where we're headed? I thought we were going to Gettysburg.

LOUIS RIEL: What made you think that?

THOMAS SCOTT: Three days ago you said, "Thomas, do you want to go to Gettysburg with me?" And I said, "Why are you asking me? Don't you hate me?" And then you said—

LOUIS RIEL: I remember what I said.

THOMAS SCOTT: What's in Reddish River? Why are we going there and not to Gettysburg, the site of the bloodiest battle of the Civil War?

LOUIS RIEL: Do you want to visit the site where history was made, or do you want to be the one to make history?

THOMAS SCOTT: I don't know. I just want to be happy. What do you want to do?

LOUIS RIEL: I don't know, Thomas. I just don't know. You see that path up ahead? If we go left, it will take us to Gettysburg. But, if we go right, it will lead us right to Reddish River. It was nary more than five or so years ago that I dreamed of the glory of that Pennsylvanian battlefield, guns ablaze, horse agallop, Lincoln's words resonating deep within my soul as the Union fights day and night for a more just world.

THOMAS SCOTT: Ooh, so you were on that side of the war.

LOUIS RIEL: Yes. Of course. What side did you think I was on?

THOMAS SCOTT: I thought you were on the same side as me, I guess.

LOUIS RIEL: A Confederate? Ha.

THOMAS SCOTT: Don't ha. They were fighting for a beautiful cause. A lost cause.

LOUIS RIEL: Lost cause? Please. That's a pseudohistorical piece of propaganda, a negationist myth.

THOMAS SCOTT: I thought they had nice architecture.

LOUIS RIEL: I expected more from you, Thomas.

THOMAS SCOTT: You did?

LOUIS RIEL: Yes, I did. Not a lot more, but . . . ever so slightly more. But I suppose we all must choose our own path. Who am I to dictate your choices?

THOMAS SCOTT: That's the nicest thing anybody has ever said to me. I'll go wherever you go, buddy. So, which way are we going?

LOUIS RIEL: Everyone expects me to go to Reddish River. They expect me to fight. But that's not me, is it? I'm just a simple poet with a great moustache. I yearn not for war. I want to be held and caressed and . . . loved.

THOMAS SCOTT: I think this is a love letter, Louis. Listen: "Our mutual friend, dear sweet Eugenia, believes we will get along swimmingly, and I agree. Oh yes, my name is Marie-Angelique. I am—"

LOUIS RIEL: What did you say?

THOMAS SCOTT: What?

LOUIS RIEL: What was that name again?

THOMAS SCOTT: Marie-Angelique? Beautiful name.

LOUIS RIEL: Before that.

THOMAS SCOTT: Oh, Eugenia? That's good too.

LOUIS RIEL: Eugenia.

THOMAS SCOTT: That's right, Eugenia. Like Eugene but with an ia.

LOUIS RIEL: Eugenia. Temptress. Seductress. Siren.

THOMAS SCOTT: Ooh, it sounds like there's a story here.

LOUIS RIEL: Shut up, Thomas.

THOMAS SCOTT: Sounds like we'll hear the story later.

LOUIS RIEL: She's in Reddish River, you say?

THOMAS SCOTT: Well, Marie-Angelique says. I'm just reading.

LOUIS RIEL: Hm. Well. Continue.

THOMAS SCOTT: "I am twenty-two years old, and a Taurus with Sun rising in Leo, so I hate change." Hey, that's interesting, I hate change too!

LOUIS RIEL: Change is the only thing we can count on. Change is a harbinger of . . . more change.

THOMAS SCOTT: Oh yeah, for sure, for sure. "And as you are a Libra on the cusp of Scorpio, I envision a thrilling meeting of the minds is fated for us." You're a Libra?

LOUIS RIEL: I don't believe in astrology . . . but I do believe in fate.

THOMAS SCOTT: "I eagerly await your arrival to our beautiful fort. I can't wait to meet you and hope I may be able to contribute meaningfully to your noble cause."

LOUIS RIEL: Is this a sign? Is this my destiny? To return to Reddish River? To fight for my people? To win back the love of my life?

THOMAS SCOTT: "Some people may call you selfish," ow, harsh but true, "but I value your devoted leadership."

LOUIS RIEL: Can I really be a great poet, a noble leader, and a formidable lover?

THOMAS SCOTT: "You are a Métis man of esteem and prestige, and I am a Métis woman of . . . well, let's just say, you could do worse." You hear that? You could do worse!

LOUIS RIEL: She could do worse. I've got poems to write . . . and a lover to woo . . . and a war to win.

THOMAS SCOTT: "Goodbye for now, and safe travels. Lots of love, Marie-Angelique! Xoxo." Aw. That's how I sign my letters too.

THOMAS preps a piece of paper, ready to respond.

All right. I'm ready. What is your response?

LOUIS RIEL: I don't have time for a response. I have a war to win.

THOMAS SCOTT: You said that already.

LOUIS RIEL: Did I? Or did you just hear me twice?

THOMAS SCOTT: Uh both?

LOUIS RIEL: Exactly.

LOUIS stands and prepares to leave.

THOMAS SCOTT: Did you decide where we are you going?

LOUIS RIEL: I'm going to Reddish River.

THOMAS SCOTT: Are you sure? But the Gettysburg ghost tour is non-refundable.

LOUIS RIEL: Gettysburg can wait. It will still be there next year.

THOMAS SCOTT: Is this about that woman? Eugenia?

LOUIS RIEL: Vixen. Minx. Jezebel. No. This is not about a woman. This is about destiny. I'm leaving at dawn.

THOMAS SCOTT: Yes, sir. And, uh, do you want me to join you, or . . . ?

LOUIS RIEL: Join me, or don't.

THOMAS SCOTT: Okay, I will!

LOUIS RIEL: Great.

LOUIS leaves with his Louis Vuitton suitcase.

THOMAS SCOTT: Reddish River. Could be fun. Could be a life out there for me. Could be land out there for me.

THOMAS rereads MARIE-ANGELIQUE's letter, silently.

And who knows, maybe even love. Maybe Louis is right. Maybe fate is real. And maybe . . . maybe she could do worse. A lot worse.

THOMAS comes up with a plan and begins to write a letter of his own.

FIVE

Back in the fort. The women are still rocking.

CECILIA: I thought it was a delightful film. After all, I love *Cats* the musical and the animal, but the proportions seemed all askew, didn't you think—

A letter drops into CECILIA's lap.

Oh! At last. News from my husband. I'm married, you see.

CECILIA casually pointedly strokes her wedding ring.

MARIE-ANGELIQUE: What's the tea?

CECILIA: He writes that William McDougall's arrival is imminent.

EUGENIA: Now there is a handsome man. No moustache. Strong fighter.

MARIE-ANGELIQUE: Where did he fight?

CECILIA: Why, Gettysburg of course.

MARIE-ANGELIQUE: Gettysburg! The bloodiest battle of the Civil War! I've always wanted to visit. Do one of those ghost tours.

EUGENIA: It would be awful if what happened there happened here.

MARIE-ANGELIQUE: Louis Riel would never let that happen. Our land will be kept healthy and safe. The water will always be fresh, and the trees will grow tall and strong, and all the animals will come back someday. We will build a new world and in this new world all the men will want to trade with you, and you will be rich, and you can bring your family down here to Reddish River!

EUGENIA: I think they like it up north, away from this European garbage fire.

MARIE-ANGELIQUE: Fires spread.

EUGENIA: Yeah. They do. And that's why it's so important /
that we—

MARIE-ANGELIQUE: Louis Riel and I . . . we didn't start the fire. It was always burning since the world's been turning, but we will endeavour until our dying day to put that fire out. If the settlers cannot live peacefully upon this land, then they should not live here at all.

CECILIA: I beg your pardon?

MARIE-ANGELIQUE: You heard me.

CECILIA: I haven't done anything wrong. It's not my fault my husband is a—well, quite frankly, I don't know what he does. I just know he's not particularly good at it. But don't put his sins on my shoulders. I thought we were friends forever. We pinky swore.

MARIE-ANGELIQUE: You're right. Sorry for being such a little bitch. The uncertainty of all of this—our room, our fort, our river, our land—is really taking a toll.

CECILIA: I accept your apology, Marie-Angelique. These are trying times. We must stick together and put our belief in the Lord our God.

CECILIA looks to the heavens and makes the sign of the cross.
MARIE-ANGELIQUE copies her, with mild apprehension. EUGENIA
follows suit, but does it purposefully wrongly, like Tom Hanks
in A League of Their Own.

MARIE-ANGELIQUE: And in these times uncertain, I endeavour to emerge as a figure of worth and esteem. But I also know that I must have a man beside me to be taken seriously. And who better than Louis Riel. Let us plan the wedding.

CECILIA: Yes, let's. Women grow by men.

EUGENIA: I grow independent and alone.

MARIE-ANGELIQUE: And I . . . grow using men to further my purpose. Is that so wrong?

CECILIA: Yes, very.   EUGENIA: It's a little manipulative but I'm honestly fine with it.

A letter drops from the sky into the lap of MARIE-ANGELIQUE.
MARIE-ANGELIQUE gasps.

MARIE-ANGELIQUE: Oh my god. Oh my god. Oh my god oh my god oh my god oh my god oh my GOD oh my god my god oh my oh my oh me oh my my god my dog my word he wrote back! He wrote me! He wrote me a letter! Louis Riel! Wrote me a letter! Louis! Riel! Rebel! Poet! Leader! Hero! Prophet! Moustache!

EUGENIA: You gonna read it or just keep saying words?

MARIE-ANGELIQUE: A letter from Reddish River's very own Che Guevara? Of course I'm going to read it.

MARIE-ANGELIQUE holds the letter for a while.

Okay, I can't, I'm too nervous! Cecilia, you do it! Do it in his voice!

CECILIA: I don't know what he sounds like.

MARIE-ANGELIQUE: Try!

CECILIA grabs the letter, the LOUIS RIEL doll, and clears her throat.

CECILIA: *(as LOUIS RIEL)* Dear Marie-Angelique,

MARIE-ANGELIQUE: Did you hear that? He called me DEAR!

CECILIA: *(as LOUIS RIEL)* Thank you so much for your warm, inspiring letter. Your observations and insights about me were / most astute.

EUGENIA: Oh my god. You're doing it wrong. He doesn't sound like that at all. Here, give it to me.

EUGENIA grabs the letter and the doll and takes a stab. It's . . . better, but I don't know if Louis himself would call it accurate.

(as LOUIS RIEL) I have never felt so wholly understood and loved for myself and not for my poetry or my moustache. It seems we have an enormous amount in common, two lost souls swimming in the same colonizer fishbowl, Roman calendar year after Roman calendar year.

EUGENIA & LOUIS RIEL: *(both as LOUIS RIEL)* Your letter came at the perfect time—just as I intend to do—to the fort I mean, not to, well, never mind—because although war is inevitable—

LOUIS RIEL & THOMAS SCOTT: *(as LOUIS RIEL and THOMAS SCOTT)*—with the stimulating support from a beautiful, powerful, Taurean with Leo ascending Métis woman such as yourself engorging my body with the white-hot heat of passion, I am confident that I can remain—

THOMAS SCOTT: *(as THOMAS SCOTT)* —erect in the face of the trials before me and protect our world from those who wish to do us harm. Upon my return to Reddish River, it would be my deepest pleasure to meet with you and see if this pulsating connection I sense between us in these letters is as real as I hope it is.

LOUIS RIEL & THOMAS SCOTT: *(as LOUIS RIEL and THOMAS SCOTT)* There is so much work to be done, Marie-Angelique.

EUGENIA & LOUIS RIEL: *(both as LOUIS RIEL)* And I have felt ever so alone.

EUGENIA & CECILIA: *(both as LOUIS RIEL)* Until now. Suddenly the world is filled with wonder and with hope.

CECILIA: *(as LOUIS RIEL)* Because suddenly the world is filled with you. Throbbingly yours,

(as CECILIA) Louis Riel. Xoxo.

MARIE-ANGELIQUE: Holy shit, what the fuck.

CECILIA: What a kind letter. He sounds lovely.

EUGENIA: Throbbingly? Pulsating? Erect? This doesn't sound like him at all. This doesn't even look like his handwriting.

MARIE-ANGELIQUE: Eugenia, important people don't write their own letters. They have less important people do that for them.

CECILIA: What will your response be?

MARIE-ANGELIQUE: "Yes! Yes, yes, yes. Yes, to all of this. Yes." Oh. Eugenia, hand me my paper and my quill.

EUGENIA: Why? It's closer to you than it is to me. Just get it yourself, it's like right there.

MARIE-ANGELIQUE begrudgingly picks up her own quill and paper.

MARIE-ANGELIQUE: Cecilia. Your penmanship is so much more distinguished than mine. Would you do me the honour of being my personal letter writer in my correspondences with Louis Riel?

CECILIA: Yes, of course. It would be my pleasure.

CECILIA prepares the quill for some hardcore letter-writing.

MARIE-ANGELIQUE: "Dear Louis Riel,

Bonjour. My heart is bursting with joy from your beautiful letter. I am utterly delighted for our upcoming meeting. I will wait patiently here in the fort for your return." Should I give him directions to find me or . . . ?

EUGENIA: No, don't give him any additional information. Let him seek you out. Men love that.

MARIE-ANGELIQUE: So wise. "I have heard tell that a rebellion is imminent, and I endeavour to support you. Don't ask me how, but I have access to many weapons. I am not like other girls, Louis. I am ready to fight. I must fight. It is my duty. This country needs a change, and I think you and I could be that change. Prime Minister John A. Macdonald—"

CECILIA: What does the A stand for?

EUGENIA: Asshole.

MARIE-ANGELIQUE: "—is a most terrible man. I can help you, Louis. I can help you help our people. I see the real you, Louis, and I find it beautiful. Respectfully yours, Marie-Angelique. Xoxo."

MARIE-ANGELIQUE waits for CECILIA to finish writing the letter.

Hurry up, hurry up. Why is it taking you so long?

CECILIA: It's the 1800s, everything takes long. I'm writing with a quill.

Beat.

. . . May I say something?

MARIE-ANGELIQUE: If you must.

CECILIA: Perhaps it would behoove you to be a touch more demure in your letter? What you're saying here could be misconstrued as treason.

MARIE-ANGELIQUE: It wouldn't be misconstrued. It is treason. I'm committing treason! Wow, Like Marie Antoinette. Mm, I love cake.

EUGENIA: She was guillotined.

MARIE-ANGELIQUE: Ugh hot.

EUGENIA: What?

CECILIA proudly holds up the letter.

CECILIA: Finished!

MARIE-ANGELIQUE seals it with a kiss.

MARIE-ANGELIQUE: Now we must ensure this letter is sent to the appropriate hands.

MARIE-ANGELIQUE is about to fling the letter high in the air, but EUGENIA stops her.

EUGENIA: No! If this letter gets into the wrong hands . . . you cannot place your trust in Canada Post. If you are formally going to align yourself with Louis Riel, you must be more careful now. There are enemies everywhere.

CECILIA grabs the letter.

CECILIA: My husband can take it and bring it east to the—

MARIE-ANGELIQUE slaps CECILIA's hand. CECILIA drops the letter.

MARIE-ANGELIQUE & EUGENIA: No!

CECILIA: Great jumping Jehoshaphat.

MARIE-ANGELIQUE: Who is Jehoshaphat?

CECILIA: The fourth king of Judah.

MARIE-ANGELIQUE: Why do you know that? You're not Jewish. This is the fur trade; nobody here is Jewish!

CECILIA: Surely some people here are Jewish.

EUGENIA: Cecilia's right.

CECILIA: I am?

EUGENIA: Yeah.

CECILIA: Wow.

EUGENIA: Jewish people have been quite instrumental / in trading, especially with overseas countries and—

CECILIA: But anyway, the point is I trust my husband with my life.

EUGENIA: Yes, but do you trust him with ours? You said it yourself, your husband hates Louis Riel.

CECILIA: He doesn't hate Louis. He just thinks that Louis Riel is a dangerous force against the righteous imperial quest to colonize Canada and free it from the shackles of the Indians.

MARIE-ANGELIQUE: Excuse me, Native Americans.

EUGENIA: Aboriginals.

MARIE-ANGELIQUE: First Nations . . . ?

EUGENIA: . . . Indigenous?

MARIE-ANGELIQUE: Ya that's good I can get on board with that.

CECILIA: Who cares? It's all just words.

EUGENIA: No offence, Cecilia, but your husband is a bit of a tool. How do you not punch him like every day?

CECILIA: In my defence, I very rarely see him. And I don't agree with him, necessarily.

   Beat.

And even if I did, you are still my dearest friends.

Beat.

Couldn't we not simply agree to disagree?

Beets.

He does strive for your safety, Marie-Angelique, and the safety of all the Métis and the Indian . . . Native . . . First Nations Aboriginal Indigenous peoples.

A triangle dings.

EUGENIA: It's that time again.

MARIE-ANGELIQUE: What is that sound?

EUGENIA: It's Matthew the Incompetent Blacksmith. It's the dinner bell. Amongst other things. Here. Give me the letter. I'll do it.

MARIE-ANGELIQUE: You will?

CECILIA: Oh, Eugenia!

EUGENIA: Yes. There's . . . there's something I need to say to him. Face to face.

MARIE-ANGELIQUE: Let me come with you.

EUGENIA: No.

MARIE-ANGELIQUE: Please. I want to get out of here. I want to be of use. I know how to start fires and I can cook a very okay bannock.

EUGENIA: No. It's too dangerous out there.

MARIE-ANGELIQUE: This is Canada. It's dangerous everywhere now, isn't it?

CECILIA coughs.

EUGENIA: Stay here. Take care of Cecilia. She's not well.

CECILIA: I'm fine!

EUGENIA: Both of you rest and conserve your strength. Be patient. That's a kind of bravery. What is coming will come, whether you race to meet it or not.

MARIE-ANGELIQUE: Eugenia, how can I ever . . . Miigwetch.

EUGENIA: I'll see you all again. Soon. Although . . . things may be different then.

Letter in hand, EUGENIA peaces the heck out. MARIE-ANGELIQUE and CECILIA sit quietly in their rocking chairs.

MARIE-ANGELIQUE: I wish I wasn't so jealous, and I know it's not very ladylike, but it's not fair. How come she gets to leave all the time and I can't even find the door?

CECILIA: There's a door?

MARIE-ANGELIQUE: There must be. How else did we get here? How else does she come and go so easily?

CECILIA: I've never thought about it before. I just thought I was probably born here. Besides, I like sitting and rocking. Although it would be interesting, wouldn't it? Walking through a door.

MARIE-ANGELIQUE: Maybe you were born here, but I wasn't. So I must have walked through a door before. But I don't remember. I wish I could remember what it was like, or where it was.

CECILIA: I'm sure you'll walk through a door again someday, Marie-Angelique, if it is what you truly want.

MARIE-ANGELIQUE: . . . I think . . . I think it is.

CECILIA: I bet Louis Riel walks through doors all the time. And Thomas Scott, too.

MARIE-ANGELIQUE: Yeah. *Yeah.* And soon, I will join him. Louis, not Thomas.

CECILIA: Yeah. *Yeah.* Well, the letter is written and on its way to its destination. And now it is time for us to perform our womanly duties and sit quietly. Oh, isn't life grand upon the banks of the Reddish River? Nothing bad could ever happen to us here.

    The women sip their tea. EUGENIA re-enters.

EUGENIA: That's weird.

CECILIA: Back so soon?

MARIE-ANGELIQUE: How long have we been drinking tea?

EUGENIA: No . . . I didn't leave.

CECILIA: Why not?

EUGENIA: I can't find the door. It's gone.

EUGENIA sits back in her chair. She rocks back and forth and back and forth and back and forth, faster and faster and faster until coming to a complete stop.

CECILIA: Hmm. Well. S'more tea?

CECILIA gives MARIE-ANGELIQUE and EUGENIA some more tea. CECILIA takes a sip of hers. She coughs.

SIX

Back with the boys, en route to the Reddish River, setting up camp for the evening.

THOMAS SCOTT: How much longer?

LOUIS RIEL: Not long.

THOMAS SCOTT: Right. I'm nervous.

LOUIS RIEL: You should be. You won't be greeted warmly.

THOMAS SCOTT: What makes you think that? The fort is full of upstanding white people like myself! And we've been exchanging the loveliest letters . . .

LOUIS RIEL: Who?

THOMAS SCOTT: Me and that girl, the one who wrote you that fan letter, Marie-Angelique.

LOUIS RIEL: What? Why?

THOMAS SCOTT: You told me to write her back, so I did.

LOUIS RIEL: I didn't tell you to do that.

THOMAS SCOTT: Yeah, you did. You said, "She could do worse." And the only thing worse than you is me. So I wrote her back.

LOUIS RIEL: That's a really sad way to think of yourself. Also, not a particularly pleasant way to describe me. She's really been writing to you? I wonder why.

THOMAS SCOTT: Well, I write great letters.

LOUIS RIEL: That's true, you do. But you shouldn't waste time with such frivolity. There are bigger problems to be dealt with.

THOMAS SCOTT: Yeah, yeah, we've all got problems. But the world doesn't just revolve around you, Louis. And weren't you just saying days ago that love matters just as much as war?

LOUIS RIEL: That was then. Things have changed. The battle draws ever closer. And yet you waste your time on letters. You're a fool.

THOMAS SCOTT: Hey! I'm really getting tired of you treating me like garbage. I'm a person, not a punching bag. Besides, has it ever occurred to you that I'm actually the one with more power here? I'm white.

LOUIS RIEL: What? I didn't notice.

THOMAS SCOTT: The government isn't the enemy, Louis. You said yourself that you love change—this is change. This is the future. Fighting against change is selfish. You're a selfish man, Louis. A mean, selfish, handsome man. And this land will be ours. It belongs to us.

LOUIS RIEL: Let me tell you something, Thomas. Something your precious Canadian government will never admit: the land belongs to itself. Not to the government or you or anyone else. I don't think it's selfish to fight for sovereignty. In fact, I believe it to be just the opposite. But thank you for calling me handsome. Now, what did these letters say?

THOMAS SCOTT: Oh, so now you want to know.

LOUIS RIEL: I'm curious. And we've got time to kill.

THOMAS SCOTT: Well, just, you know, that you're on your way to Reddish River and that you are thrilled to finally meet her after all this time.

LOUIS RIEL: *I'm* thrilled to meet her?

THOMAS SCOTT: Yeah, see, I may have signed the letter in your name, for gravitas and such. Which, in retrospect, I regret because I actually find her very charming, even if she is partially a savage.

LOUIS RIEL: So what are you going to do when you meet her?

THOMAS SCOTT: I dunno. I thought maybe you could . . . help? Introduce us? Put in a good word for me? I really think she may be able to help your cause.

LOUIS RIEL: Which begs the question, why are you helping my cause? We have completely opposite goals and political beliefs. And it doesn't benefit you.

THOMAS SCOTT: Well, because. Because we're friends. And friends help each other.

LOUIS RIEL: We're not friends, Thomas. We're just people who hang out sometimes. You're a racist Irish Protestant. I'm a Métis Catholic.

THOMAS SCOTT: So? We're like those dudes from *The Fox and the Hound*. One was a fox and one was a hound and they were different, but they were still friends.

LOUIS RIEL: Yeah, until they grew up.

THOMAS SCOTT: What happened when they grew up?

LOUIS RIEL: Didn't you watch the movie?

THOMAS SCOTT: Well part of it. It was late. I fell asleep. Point is, we all want the same thing, don't we? Freedom, safety, a place to call home.

LOUIS RIEL: I don't know if this country is big enough for all of us. But you're right . . . Reddish River is my home. I am going back to mine, and I suggest you return to yours.

THOMAS SCOTT: To Ireland? I can't. There's nothing left there.

LOUIS RIEL: Then you understand what I'm fighting for. Go home and fight for your own country.

THOMAS SCOTT: Who put you in charge? Why do you get to make the rules?

LOUIS RIEL: Someone has to. Someone has to stand up to this "Canada" and to John A. Macdonald and to William McDougall . . . and to you.

THOMAS SCOTT: They're Scottish. I'm nothing like them.

LOUIS RIEL: Prove it. Declare, publicly, whose side you're on. Demand restitution. Demand action. Stand up to those people who you say you're nothing like.

Silence.

THOMAS SCOTT: . . . I don't see how that would help.

LOUIS RIEL: Hm. Right. Right. The Reddish River will never be your home, Thomas. It is ours. And we won't let you take it away from us.

THOMAS SCOTT: Louis, bro, please.

LOUIS RIEL: *Au revoir,* old sport. See you on the battlefield.

THOMAS SCOTT: Not if I see you there first. Old sport.

LOUIS exits. THOMAS begins to write another letter.

"Dear Prime Minister Macdonald,

Louis Riel is on his way to Reddish River. He plans to lead the next rebellion. Send every support you can. We must do what is right and free Canada from the Indian problem. They refuse to make way for expansion . . . and refuse to make way for the future. And we are the future. And we will prevail. Throbbingly—no—Sincerely, Thomas Scott. Xoxo. No. Just Thomas Scott. Period."

THOMAS SCOTT seals up the letter and ships it via FedEx.

SEVEN

The fort.

MARIE-ANGELIQUE: Someone will come. Louis Riel will come. I know he will. If not for me, then for Reddish River. He will seize the fort and will burn this whole place to the ground and then we will be free.

EUGENIA: Or dead.

MARIE-ANGELIQUE: I'd rather be dead than stuck in here. Don't worry, Eugenia, soon we will be under the magnanimous rule of a great, handsome Métis leader who will protect our way of life and ensure that white settlers and Ottawa surveyors and their docile, useless wives / do not scorch this scared land!

CECILIA: Hold on, what the hell are you—

CECILIA stands, then coughs, then sits.

MARIE-ANGELIQUE: No offence. Soon we will be free. Soon Louis Riel will return.

CECILIA: But if he has come to seize the fort . . . what about my husband? My children? What about me?

MARIE-ANGELIQUE: What about you? Why is everything always about you?

CECILIA: It isn't! But we're people too. What will he do to us in the name of protecting you?

MARIE-ANGELIQUE: I don't know.

EUGENIA: The rebellion is making a list of rights to protect the land. He intends to create a provisional government.

CECILIA: What's that?

MARIE-ANGELIQUE: A government just for Reddish River. A government separate from Canada rule and separate from that mouthbreather John A. Macdonald!

CECILIA: So, we will all be separated?

MARIE-ANGELIQUE: . . . Maybe? I don't know. I'm not a politician. I'm just a beautiful young woman trapped in a fort, hidden away from the world, struck down in the prime of life.

CECILIA coughs several times, more strenuously now.

Maybe you should go to a doctor.

CECILIA: I can't go to a doctor. We're trapped here.

MARIE-ANGELIQUE: Louis Riel will rescue us.

CECILIA: And then divide us. We don't need more division and separation; we need to come together and stop dwelling on the past. Did you learn nothing from your mother?

MARIE-ANGELIQUE: Ugh my mother.

CECILIA: We are just women. Politics is none of our business.

MARIE-ANGELIQUE: But it is! It is our business. These are our lives. And now Ottawa has sent surveyors here to take our land away and claim it for their own. This is what the Canadian Party wants.

This is what your husband wants, what your precious Thomas Scott wants. And honestly? It kind of sounds like what you want too.

CECILIA: I just don't want to live in fear for my life all the time.

EUGENIA: Yeah, that'd be nice.

CECILIA: That sounded a little pointed.

EUGENIA: It was.

CECILIA: Has Ottawa really sent a surveyor?

EUGENIA: The land won't measure up itself.

MARIE-ANGELIQUE: They'll probably do it in squares too. Ugh.

CECILIA: What's wrong with squares?

MARIE-ANGELIQUE: The French do it properly. Seigneurially.

CECILIA: What's that?

EUGENIA: It's a bougie way of saying rectangle.

CECILIA: Surely there is a fair way to lay claim to the free land. If you legally obtain a title to a plot, what reason could they have to take that away? Just divide it all in equal parts and—

MARIE-ANGELIQUE: This is the earth, Cecilia, not a cake. The idea that you can just own a piece of it is so freaking . . . wh*te.

CECILIA: Must we resort to name-calling?

MARIE-ANGELIQUE: That's not an insult. That's just a descriptor.

CECILIA: Well, you keep implying that I'm racist when clearly you're actually the one racist towards me.

EUGENIA: That's not a thing.

CECILIA: We're all just people. Who cares where we come from or what colour our skin is? I don't see myself as white, just like I don't see you as brownish or you as fairly pale but with a summer tan. Besides, your father is white.

MARIE-ANGELIQUE: So what?

CECILIA: So, whatever you're blaming me for is part of your culture, too. You benefit from the same things I benefit from. You purposely choose to separate yourself and draw attention to yourself, but you could choose otherwise. You could choose safety; you could be like me. Stay quiet, stay out of the way, and this will all just blow over. You can get married, and have children, and we can be friends forever, like we always planned.

CECILIA holds out her pinky.

MARIE-ANGELIQUE: I can't. Maybe once I could, but now . . . the things I've read in these letters. I understand so much more now. And I just can't pretend anymore. I stand with Louis Riel. I stand with the Métis people. I publicly denounce the survey and the theft of our land. I demand retribution for all of us and I will be on the battlefields of the rebellion alongside my people.

CECILIA drops her pinky.

CECILIA: Well. At least I still have a friend in Eugenia.

EUGENIA: Uummmmmmhmmm. As much as it pains me to say so since I don't particularly respect him . . . I too stand with Louis Riel.

CECILIA: Oh. Wonderful. This is just fantastic.

MARIE-ANGELIQUE: Cecilia, be our friend. Support us. Speak to your husband. Fight with us.

CECILIA: I care about you both so much. I want us all to be safe and free. And so . . . and so . . . and so . . . and so I support you both but shall refrain from making a decision either way until I better understand the situation.

MARIE-ANGELIQUE: Until you better benefit from a side, you mean.

CECILIA: These are treacherous times. We all must do what it takes to survive.

> *No talking. No rocking. A letter arrives and falls in CECILIA's lap. She opens it. She reads it. She closes it.*

Hm. It is from my husband. Louis Riel has been declared leader of the provisional government.

MARIE-ANGELIQUE: Yes! I knew it!

CECILIA: And William McDougall has been declared first lieutenant-governor of the territory.

MARIE-ANGELIQUE: Frick.

CECILIA: What does this mean for us?

MARIE-ANGELIQUE: There is no us. Not anymore.

EUGENIA: McDougall is an expansionist. He plans to marginalize the influence of the Métis and the Natives to get what he wants.

MARIE-ANGELIQUE: Land.

EUGENIA: Power.

MARIE-ANGELIQUE: What's the difference?

CECILIA: Maybe he just wants to do what he believes is right.

EUGENIA: He's going to kill us.

CECILIA gasps.

MARIE-ANGELIQUE: She means her and I, not you.

CECILIA: Yes, I realize that. I was exhibiting care about your fate. For some reason.

MARIE-ANGELIQUE: I can't let this happen, Eugenia. It would break my mother's heart. This isn't what she fought for. This isn't why she brought me here, or why she left me behind. We must find a way out of this room. We have to fight. There has to be another door. Or a window. Or a loose floorboard that leads to a secret tunnel. Or . . . I wonder what's behind all these portraits.

EUGENIA: Shall we find out?

MARIE-ANGELIQUE: I think we shall. Cecilia? Are you going to help us?

CECILIA: Shan't. It's impossible. I have work to do.

CECILIA begins to make a new doll.

The portraits of the men begin to moan and wail. A baby begins to cry. The triangle dings and dings.

MARIE-ANGELIQUE steps closer to the wall. She reaches her hand up and caresses a portrait of someone. The portrait smiles. She leans in, as if to kiss it. Then she rips its head off and holds it in her hand. The portrait blinks. A scream forms on its face but no sound comes out. She eats the head and continues ripping portraits off the wall.

After a few moments, EUGENIA *joins.*

Stop. Stop it. You're going to ruin everything.

When the last two portraits—those of THOMAS SCOTT *and* LOUIS RIEL—*are the only ones remaining, a window is revealed. Beyond the window is something similar to a silent night, illuminated by only the moon and a handful of stars. But it's not night and it's not really outside.*

MARIE-ANGELIQUE: Oh wow. Look. The moon.

EUGENIA: Take this. You might need it.

EUGENIA puts a necklace around MARIE-ANGELIQUE'S *neck.*

MARIE-ANGELIQUE: Aren't you coming?

CECILIA coughs.

EUGENIA: Someone must stay here and take care of Cecilia. She may be on the wrong side but she's still our friend. And she is very sick.

CECILIA: Really, I'm fine.

EUGENIA: Go. And give this to Louis, if you. . . when you. . . find him. And don't forget about us. That can happen out there. Goodbye, Marie-Angelique.

MARIE-ANGELIQUE: I'll be back soon, I promise.

MARIE-ANGELIQUE climbs through the window. Behind her, it slams shut and disappears.

EIGHT

MARIE-ANGELIQUE walks through the fort. A fire burns. There are signs of life, but no people. It's unsettling. A little ominous. But certainly an interesting experience.

MARIE-ANGELIQUE: Hello? Is anybody out here?

THOMAS SCOTT appears.

THOMAS SCOTT: Excuse me, miss.

MARIE-ANGELIQUE: Ahh! Stand back, I've got a gun!

MARIE-ANGELIQUE picks up a stick and waves it around.

THOMAS SCOTT: I think that's a stick.

MARIE-ANGELIQUE: Yeah. It is. It is. I panicked. I'm sorry. I don't have any money and I'm not worth murdering or kidnapping, nobody would pay for me or come looking for me, so you should probably just go find someone else to do whatever to, okay, sir?

THOMAS SCOTT: I don't mean any harm. I'm looking for someone, a woman who lives in this fort.

MARIE-ANGELIQUE: Oh, you must mean Cecilia. She's—

THOMAS SCOTT: I'm looking for a Marie-Angelique.

MARIE-ANGELIQUE: *Pour moi?*

THOMAS SCOTT: Possibly. Is that you? Is this your letter?

MARIE-ANGELIQUE: How did you get that? What have you done with Louis Riel? Tell me. Tell me or I'll shoot.

THOMAS SCOTT: That's still just a stick. Look, I just want to find her to talk. I really liked her letters. So, if you know where she is, I would appreciate it if you would let me know.

MARIE-ANGELIQUE: Maybe she's here. But maybe she's confused about why you have those letters and maybe she would appreciate you telling her why you have them.

THOMAS SCOTT: Louis was . . . is . . . a friend of mine. I transcribed his letters for him. Uh, I'm looking for him right now, as a matter of fact, to, uh, return these to him.

MARIE-ANGELIQUE: I'm looking for him too. I have to warn him. The Canadian Party is on its way and they'll kill him if they find him.

THOMAS SCOTT: Oh, that sucks. Um, maybe we can look together.

MARIE-ANGELIQUE: Sure. Okay. I am Marie-Angelique, by the way. I've been exchanging letters with Louis for some time now. I'm his biggest fan and I want to help in any way I can.

THOMAS SCOTT: We'll find him. I promise.

THOMAS SCOTT and MARIE-ANGELIQUE begin to walk.

MARIE-ANGELIQUE: It's cold.

THOMAS SCOTT puts his coat around her. It's thrilling and so romantic!

Merci. I should have brought my furs. I have many. I haven't been outside in a long time.

THOMAS SCOTT: Where *have* you been?

MARIE-ANGELIQUE: Indoors. Over there. Or maybe . . . over there. Somewhere. In a room with two other women. We each have a rocking chair and a teacup. It's humble but it's home. Or, well, it *was* home. Where's home for you?

THOMAS SCOTT: I . . . don't know. I guess that's sort of what I'm looking for.

MARIE-ANGELIQUE: I feel that. I've never really felt at home here. I was born in the woods but was sent away to learn how to be a proper lady. I'm afraid I'm not a very good one. I have too many opinions and I can't even sew.

THOMAS SCOTT: Opinions are good. Some people don't have any. I didn't, for a long time. Or maybe I did, but they were born from ignorance and not from wisdom.

MARIE-ANGELIQUE: And your new opinions? Are they wise?

THOMAS SCOTT: Not wise but necessary.

MARIE-ANGELIQUE: Right. Right.

> *MARIE-ANGELIQUE trips and stumbles. The necklace falls off, but she doesn't notice. THOMAS SCOTT catches MARIE-ANGELIQUE and pockets the necklace.*

So you're a friend of Louis's?

THOMAS SCOTT: Definitely. Really close friends. Best friends, really. Although, I've always thought that best friend was more of a tier than any individual person.

MARIE-ANGELIQUE: . . . That's what I've always believed, too.

THOMAS SCOTT: Really?

MARIE-ANGELIQUE: Yeah. You look so familiar to me . . . what did you say your name was?

THOMAS SCOTT: I didn't. It's . . . well my friends call me Tom.

MARIE-ANGELIQUE: Tom. That's a nice name.

THOMAS SCOTT: So is Marie-Angelique. It's . . . angelic.

MARIE-ANGELIQUE: *Merci.* I was named after my paternal grand-mother. She was from Paris. Have you ever been?

THOMAS SCOTT: To Paris? Oh, no, not me. Been to London once or twice. But, nah, I'm just a small-town kid from Ireland.

MARIE-ANGELIQUE: Oh, I thought I detected a slight accent. Wait. Tom . . . from Ireland . . . your face is so familiar . . . and your hair . . . left-side part—I know you. You were on our wall, next to Louis and Gabriel Dumont and Keanu. You're Thomas Scott.

THOMAS SCOTT: I was on your wall?

MARIE-ANGELIQUE: Racist. Irish. Protestant. Thomas Scott. That's you—you're him, aren't you?

THOMAS SCOTT: Yes. I am he.

MARIE-ANGELIQUE: You're not a friend of Louis's at all.

THOMAS SCOTT: I was, once. But not anymore.

MARIE-ANGELIQUE: You're going to kill him, aren't you?

THOMAS SCOTT: I'm just following orders. I had to make a choice. We are fighting for the future, Marie-Angelique. We are fighting for a better Canada.

MARIE-ANGELIQUE: Better for who? Because it's certainly not better for him or for me.

MARIE-ANGELIQUE takes off THOMAS SCOTT's jacket, throws it to the ground, and stomps on it.

THOMAS SCOTT: Hey, that's not cool.

MARIE-ANGELIQUE: You know what isn't cool, Thomas? Genocide.

THOMAS SCOTT: Okay, yeah, I know that. I'm not saying genocide is cool. Although if now is the right time I might suggest that you're being kind of racist / too right now, assuming just because I'm white that I'm—

MARIE-ANGELIQUE: What? No. How? What? No. What? Shut up. I'm leaving.

THOMAS SCOTT: Leaving? Without . . . this?

THOMAS SCOTT holds up the necklace.

MARIE-ANGELIQUE: Give that back. It's mine.

THOMAS SCOTT: Not until you admit that it's bad out here for all of us right now.

MARIE-ANGELIQUE: Okay, sure. But we, me and you, you and I? Do NOT experience that badness in the same way. I'm not privileged like—

THOMAS SCOTT: I don't know if I'd call myself privileged—

MARIE-ANGELIQUE: You don't have to. I'm calling you privileged.

THOMAS SCOTT: And that hurts my feelings, being insulted like that.

MARIE-ANGELIQUE: It's not meant to be an insult—it's just a fact.

THOMAS SCOTT: I'm a good person, Marie-Angelique. I want the same thing you do; I want to find a place where I belong and—

MARIE-ANGELIQUE: Then go back to Ireland, Thomas! Go anywhere else! Why here? Why do you need to take this from us? Why do you need everything?

THOMAS SCOTT: I don't want everything; I just want something. There's nothing here for Irish people either—no jobs, no housing . . . I want a better life, one where I don't have to prove every day I belong here and deserve to be treated with respect.

MARIE-ANGELIQUE: Tell me, Thomas. What's your zodiac sign?

THOMAS SCOTT: I don't know.

MARIE-ANGELIQUE: What's your date of birth?

THOMAS SCOTT: January first.

MARIE-ANGELIQUE: A Capricorn. Well. From one fixed Earth sign to another, one that understands your desire for stability, I have to say that although I understand where you're coming from, and although I empathize . . . I expected better from you.

THOMAS SCOTT: Really?

MARIE-ANGELIQUE: Yeah, I guess I did. Call me naive, but I expect people to be actually decent, to be compassionate, to acknowledge the reality—the freedoms and the limits of their lived experience—and not be garbage for some reason. Saying it out loud it does sound stupid.

THOMAS SCOTT: Maybe that's your problem. High expectations.

MARIE-ANGELIQUE: Excsqueeze me?

THOMAS SCOTT: What do you expect will happen when you find Louis Riel? Louis is a delusional coward. He can't lead a rebellion. He can't even write a good poem. Or his own letters, for that matter.

LOUIS RIEL enters.

LOUIS RIEL: Why don't you say that to my face, Thomas Scott?

THOMAS SCOTT: All right, I will, Louis Riel.

MARIE-ANGELIQUE: Louis! It's me! Marie-Angelique!

THOMAS SCOTT: Your poems are garbage and so are you.

MARIE-ANGELIQUE: I actually don't think they're that bad—

LOUIS RIEL: So you're the poor girl who has been exchanging letters with the late, great Mr. Scott here, hmm?

MARIE-ANGELIQUE: I what? Ew? Oh. No. Ew. You mean you didn't . . . You weren't the . . . oh. Oh no. Barf.

THOMAS SCOTT: That's very rude.

MARIE-ANGELIQUE: You tricked me.

THOMAS SCOTT: No, I didn't. Well, yes, I did, at first, but didn't you feel a spark? I know I did. And I came here to find you because I thought we could . . . we might . . .

MARIE-ANGELIQUE: Ew, Thomas. No, Thomas.

THOMAS SCOTT: I was being sincere when I said I really enjoyed talking to you.

LOUIS RIEL: And did you also enjoy the words of our friend Thomas Scott here, Marie-Angelique?

MARIE-ANGELIQUE: No. Absolutely not.

THOMAS SCOTT: That's not what your letters said!

MARIE-ANGELIQUE: That's because I thought I was writing to Louis!

THOMAS SCOTT: But they were my words! My feelings! My poetry!

MARIE-ANGELIQUE: But not your name. Not your face. Not the truth.

LOUIS RIEL: I told you it would never work, old sport. Better just surrender now and—

THOMAS SCOTT grabs MARIE-ANGELIQUE's stick and holds it against her head.

THOMAS SCOTT: Come any closer and I'll shoot.

LOUIS RIEL: That's a stick.

THOMAS SCOTT: I'll kill her. I will.

LOUIS RIEL: Go ahead. Kill her.

MARIE-ANGELIQUE: Hey! I'm on your side!

LOUIS RIEL: Sorry, but I don't know you. And there are always casualties in war.

MARIE-ANGELIQUE: The Louis Riel I know would never be so uncaring.

THOMAS SCOTT: That's because the Louis Riel you know is me!

MARIE-ANGELIQUE: Oh, god. I've been so stupid. Eugenia / was right. You're nothing like—

LOUIS RIEL: Eugenia? Where is she?

MARIE-ANGELIQUE: She's still inside. She gave me this letter to give to you, if I found you.

> *MARIE-ANGELIQUE gives LOUIS RIEL the letter. He reads it in silence. Then he picks up a stick.*

LOUIS RIEL: Let her go or I'll shoot.

MARIE-ANGELIQUE: Oh, thank god. Okay, so now you both have sticks. That's kind of . . . kind of hot.

> *LOUIS RIEL and THOMAS SCOTT get in a stick gun fight. It starts out silly but grows increasingly serious. There's lots of ad libbing. It ends with LOUIS capturing THOMAS. THOMAS drops the stick and MARIE-ANGELIQUE picks it up.*

LOUIS RIEL: Come along, Thomas Scott. The time has come for you to die.

THOMAS SCOTT: I die with honour. I die with dignity. I die with—

LOUIS RIEL: Shh. No more words. Thank you, Marie-Angelique, for all your assistance.

MARIE-ANGELIQUE: I didn't really do anything.

LOUIS RIEL: You delivered this letter. And, in a sense, you delivered me.

MARIE-ANGELIQUE: Did she warn you? That the enemies are coming? Or, rather, I suppose, that they're already here . . .

LOUIS RIEL: Yes. She did warn me. Amongst other things. And yes, in many ways Thomas Scott is my enemy . . . but I've always believed that the enemy of my enemy is my friend. And when you think about it like that, in many ways, we have been friends, haven't we, old sport?

THOMAS SCOTT: Well, I—

LOUIS RIEL: Shh.

LOUIS muzzles THOMAS.

MARIE-ANGELIQUE: What else do you believe in?

LOUIS RIEL: I believe in fate. I believe in the land. I believe in the Métis people. I believe in you.

MARIE-ANGELIQUE: I've been waiting for you for so long. My friends are still trapped in a room here in the fort and I've prayed and prayed that you would find us and free us.

LOUIS RIEL: How did you get out here?

MARIE-ANGELIQUE: I climbed through a window.

LOUIS RIEL: Ah. Good girl.

MARIE-ANGELIQUE: I love you.

LOUIS RIEL: That's the only kind of freedom that counts—the kind you make for yourself. Now, Thomas and I must be off.

MARIE-ANGELIQUE: Take me with you? I can fight.

LOUIS RIEL: I work alone.

MARIE-ANGELIQUE: I'll be quiet. I'll bring snacks.

LOUIS RIEL: I subsist solely on the blood of my enemies.

MARIE-ANGELIQUE: I can accommodate dietary restrictions.

LOUIS RIEL: I have been chosen.

MARIE-ANGELIQUE: By whom?

LOUIS RIEL: God. I am the prophet of the new world. I can hear them now. The bells, the angels. Do you hear them? The footfalls. The horsemen.

MARIE-ANGELIQUE: But aren't you going to help my friends? What about Eugenia? And Cecilia? She's very sick.

LOUIS RIEL: Eugenia and I are . . . it's over.

MARIE-ANGELIQUE: But we need to rescue them.

LOUIS RIEL: Rescue you them yourself.

MARIE-ANGELIQUE: Your tone was kind of flippant and dismissive but I still feel empowered. So I will. I will rescue them.

LOUIS RIEL: The woods are on fire. The sky burns. We are where the past and the future meet . . . and I am the One. Farewell.

MARIE-ANGELIQUE: *Au revoir.*

LOUIS RIEL exits with THOMAS SCOTT. They disappear into the darkness. MARIE-ANGELIQUE begins to walk back towards where she came from. Suddenly, a gunshot is heard, followed by a scream. Gunshot. Scream. Walking. Again and again. Over and over. Then she finds the window.

NINE

MARIE-ANGELIQUE crawls through the window. It's the same room, the same place, but now there's a breeze . . . and clouds . . . and the moon . . . and hope. And CECILIA has just finished making a new doll.

CECILIA: Finished!

She hands it to EUGENIA.

EUGENIA: Gabriel Dumont! Aw, you shouldn't have.

MARIE-ANGELIQUE clears her throat.

CECILIA: Oh! Hello!

EUGENIA: Welcome home.

CECILIA: We thought you were never coming back.

MARIE-ANGELIQUE: How long was I gone?

CECILIA: A year or two? It seemed like forever.

MARIE-ANGELIQUE: It felt like a minute. Why did nobody come looking for me?

CECILIA: Yours is not the only life at stake. Count your blessings that yours was not a life lost. My husband and Thomas Scott were not so lucky.

EUGENIA: It's not her fault, Cecilia. Louis had to set an example.

CECILIA: With my husband? With Thomas? He was so handsome.

MARIE-ANGELIQUE: He was very handsome, Cecilia, you're right. But Louis had to show the government that we are to be taken seriously.

CECILIA: What will I do without a husband? What will my children do without their father?

MARIE-ANGELIQUE: I'm sorry. I don't know.

CECILIA: What about our pinky swears? What about our pact? What about our friendship?

MARIE-ANGELIQUE: Louis said that sometimes the enemy of our enemy is our friend.

CECILIA: I am your friend, not your enemy.

MARIE-ANGELIQUE: In many ways, you are my enemy. But you shouldn't be. I don't want you to be. And if you believe we all deserve to live peacefully on this land, then you are also my friend.

CECILIA: I do believe that. I do. I don't want to be your enemy either.

MARIE-ANGELIQUE: Then there is work to be done. We must make our own way now . . . for no man will save us. We do not need to be saved. But we must keep working. And we must do it together. Agreed?

CECILIA: Agreed.

EUGENIA: Agreed. That's kind of what I've been saying the whole time anyway.

The three women pinky swear and write three new letters.

Dear Louis,

MARIE-ANGELIQUE: Dear Louis,

CECILIA: Dear Louis,

EUGENIA: Remember the wisdom of your ancestors. Remember the lessons of your forefathers.

MARIE-ANGELIQUE: It was so nice to meet you the other day.

CECILIA: My name is Cecilia. You murdered my husband. And Thomas Scott, the handsome Irishman.

MARIE-ANGELIQUE: I'm embarrassed by what I wrote you before and wish to apologize.

CECILIA: But perhaps not everything is quite as it seems.

EUGENIA: "Quit your bitchin' and start *miigwitchin'*," an ancient meme.

MARIE-ANGELIQUE: I created an idea of you inside my head, and it turned out to be untrue.

CECILIA: Perhaps we all want to be safe, and free.

MARIE-ANGELIQUE: Maybe you aren't who I thought you were . . . but that's okay. I don't know if I'm who I thought I was either.

EUGENIA: It's a funny thing these days . . . nobody seems to know where they belong.

CECILIA: Do remember, Louis, as you well know as a devout Catholic, that the Lord will have the final say.

EUGENIA: Even the muskrats are confused and don't know where to go.

MARIE-ANGELIQUE: I did not always live in this fort. I was born in the woods. I loved the woods. And then my mother, she . . . I couldn't forgive her for what she did.

CECILIA: Don't become so involved with the details that you can no longer see the forest for the trees.

MARIE-ANGELIQUE: I thought it was a choice. I couldn't forgive her for letting them take me.

EUGENIA: But I'm rooting for ya, old sport. And, truly, it wasn't you. It was me. I promise.

MARIE-ANGELIQUE: Fight for us, Louis. Keep fighting and don't ever stop. I'll join you when I can. I'll find my own way out. Whether that's tomorrow or a hundred years from now.

CECILIA: Evil is inevitable. But us Women of the Fur Trade are indefatigable.

EUGENIA: Throbbingly yours, your platonic friend, Eugenia.

CECILIA: Curtly but daintily, Cecilia.

MARIE-ANGELIQUE: Sincerely, Marie-Angelique.

The three women seal up their letters and toss them high in the air. CECILIA begins to cough.

EUGENIA: Oh, Cecilia . . .

CECILIA: Nothing serious. Don't worry about me.

MARIE-ANGELIQUE: Come on. We must go.

CECILIA: No. Not me. I have always been happy here in the fort. I must stay here with my family. Come what may.

MARIE-ANGELIQUE: Oh, Cecilia. I shall miss you very much.

EUGENIA: You're a good friend, Cecilia. Now, before we go, perhaps we could have one last cup of tea?

CECILIA: I must confess something.

MARIE-ANGELIQUE: What is it?

CECILIA: There is no tea. There was never any tea. The tea was a lie.

MARIE-ANGELIQUE: Yeah. We already knew that, honey.

EUGENIA: Come on, Marie-Angelique. It's time to go.

MARIE-ANGELIQUE: Where did the window go? It was right here. It was just here only moments ago. Now we're trapped again.

EUGENIA: Don't panic. We'll find another way out.

MARIE-ANGELIQUE: Okay.

And a letter falls from the sky again and into CECILIA's *lap.*

EUGENIA: Oh! A letter.

CECILIA: From?

EUGENIA: One guess.

ALL: Louis Riel.

LOUIS RIEL: Dear Women of the Fur Trade,

Thank you for your letters. I was ever so pleased to hear from all of you and would like to inform you that, yes, it is I writing this. It was even wonderful to hear from you, Eugenia, who broke my heart so many years ago. It has been so long since we last made sweet, sweet love on the banks of the River Red where the beaver makes its dam and the children frolic innocently amongst the tall grasses and the wood ticks. So much has changed, Eugenia. I've changed. I am married now. My wife, Marguerite, so hot, and I love her an appropriate amount for the time period. And I have children, Jean-Louis and Marie-Angelique—truly a beautiful name, inspired by one of my greatest fans—

MARIE-ANGELIQUE smiles.

—the loves of my life, after rebellion, resistance, and destroying the lives of the colonizers of our land. A close fourth place for my focus and attention. I will keep fighting, as you requested. And I await all of your faces, and all of your strength, on the battlefield beside me. RIEL OUT.

Inside the letter is a necklace. CECILIA hands it to MARIE-ANGELIQUE. MARIE-ANGELIQUE holds it in her hand.

EUGENIA: There will be a rebellion west of us now. The territories there saw what Louis Riel did for us. Now they demand the same from him, for themselves.

MARIE-ANGELIQUE: He succeeded here, and he will succeed out west. With our help he cannot fail.

EUGENIA: I imagine he will petition the government. He will outline the grievances and neglect the territories continue to suffer in this fight between the Indians, the Métis, and the settlers.

MARIE-ANGELIQUE: Fuck the settlers.

CECILIA coughs.

MARIE-ANGELIQUE: Oh gosh, sorry. Sorry. The enemy of my enemy is my friend, pinky swear, all that, yes.

EUGENIA: The settlers are important. The government will listen to their concerns. They won't listen to ours. It was foolish to believe they ever would. Louis will need the support of all of us and all of our communities. Ottawa has disrespected our treaty agreements, and stolen our bannock recipes, and wears our regalia as Halloween costumes. I cannot abide any of it. We must help.

MARIE-ANGELIQUE: But the window is gone. There's no way out. We've looked.

EUGENIA: Then we must do what we can from here. I will send word home.

MARIE-ANGELIQUE: As will I.

CECILIA: As will I.

The three women pen their last three letters, ever. I promise.

Dear Mother,

EUGENIA: Dear Mother,

MARIE-ANGELIQUE: Dear Mother,

CECILIA: I am writing to you about a matter of dire importance.

MARIE-ANGELIQUE: My name is Marie-Angelique, and I am your daughter.

EUGENIA: To whomever is reading this, please read it aloud.

CECILIA: My friends and I need our family's help.

MARIE-ANGELIQUE: Do you even remember me?

EUGENIA: I am losing our language and can only communicate in English now.

CECILIA: We are trapped in a fort, and they are losing their land, and their people are dying at our own hands.

MARIE-ANGELIQUE: The last memory I have of you was your turned back as they took me away.

EUGENIA: That's what you get for spending too much time in the forts. Tell my mother we require help.

CECILIA: Dying at your hands, and the hands of our people.

MARIE-ANGELIQUE: Did you not want me? Or was this your way of giving me a better life?

CECILIA: But I am not here for shame or guilt. The Lord will have his way. Justice will be swift with those who betray God and his nations.

MARIE-ANGELIQUE: I didn't need a better life. I needed my family. A man named Louis Riel . . .

EUGENIA: He is fighting for us.

CECILIA: I urge you to reconsider your position and send aid. If not for them, then for me, your daughter, as I am very ill, and my time here is limited. And in that limited time, my deepest wish is for me and my friends to be free.

MARIE-ANGELIQUE: He is fighting for us. So that mothers will never again have to give up their children. So that we may all grow up on healthy land with healthy spirits.

ALL: Rally those you can. Please send them here.

EUGENIA: Eugenia.

CECILIA: Cecilia.

MARIE-ANGELIQUE: Marie-Angelique.

> *The three women seal up their three letters and toss them into the air for the last time. MARIE-ANGELIQUE puts on her mother's necklace. Dozens of letters fall from the sky, like snowflakes or raindrops. MARIE-ANGELIQUE picks up a letter and reads it.*

Louis Riel has petitioned the Canadian government, to no avail.

> *CECILIA picks up a letter and reads it.*

CECILIA: His tactics have grown militant and aggressive and is surely not to be tolerated much longer.

> *EUGENIA picks up a letter and reads it.*

EUGENIA: His mind deteriorates.

> *CECILIA picks up a letter and reads it.*

CECILIA: He has visions.

> *MARIE-ANGELIQUE picks up a letter and reads it.*

MARIE-ANGELIQUE: He believes himself to be a prophet.

EUGENIA picks up a letter and reads it.

EUGENIA: Armed conflict in Saskatchewan Territory.

CECILIA picks up a letter and reads it.

CECILIA: The settlers have revoked their support.

MARIE-ANGELIQUE picks up a letter and reads it.

MARIE-ANGELIQUE: The Métis troops have been defeated by the government.

EUGENIA picks up a letter and reads it.

EUGENIA: Louis Riel has been arrested.

CECILIA picks up a letter and reads it.

CECILIA: Ottawa demands his execution.

EUGENIA picks up a letter and reads it.

EUGENIA: Guilty.

MARIE-ANGELIQUE: A retrial. He must demand a retrial.

CECILIA picks up a letter and reads it.

CECILIA: Denied.

EUGENIA: "He shall die though every dog in Quebec bark in his favour."

A full moon—a red moon—appears low in the sky. The women howl at it like dogs. Its light directs them to this spot, here and now, where the nation's biggest celebrity is about to meet his fate. Today is the day that LOUIS RIEL *dies, but today is just the beginning.*

TEN

CECILIA, EUGENIA, and MARIE-ANGELIQUE kneel to pray. They
each make the sign of the cross. EUGENIA does this badly.

CECILIA: In the name of the Father, the Son, and the Holy Ghost.

MARIE-ANGELIQUE: Are you there, God? It's me, Marie-Angelique.

EUGENIA: Sup.

CECILIA: I pray for your divine forgiveness.

MARIE-ANGELIQUE: I don't know if you're real, but . . .

EUGENIA: Um, do I just ask you for what I want?

CECILIA: On behalf of myself, my husband, and Louis Riel.

MARIE-ANGELIQUE: I endeavour to be prime minister now, a person
with purpose, not merely the wife of a purposeful man.

EUGENIA: Is that how this works?

MARIE-ANGELIQUE: I ask for your help, if you are there. If you're
listening.

CECILIA: I feel weaker every day, but I shall not waste prayers on myself.

MARIE-ANGELIQUE: Please let Louis through the gates and into
heaven, if that's a thing you do.

EUGENIA: I want you to be nice to my friend Louis. He's done some real dope shit. I think you'd be proud, if you're . . . well, I don't know your political affiliations / so . . .

MARIE-ANGELIQUE: He has a good heart, and a noble mind.

CECILIA: I pray for the divine forgiveness of my husband and the forgiveness of my friends.

MARIE-ANGELIQUE: I shall never forgive our oppressors.

EUGENIA: Forgiveness is not ours to give.

MARIE-ANGELIQUE: I'd like to ask you about rigging elections.

CECILIA: And a final prayer for Louis Riel.

MARIE-ANGELIQUE: But this seems like the wrong time.

EUGENIA: He is on his journey home.

> *The LOUIS RIEL doll—and LOUIS RIEL himself—walks to the gallows. He holds a silver cross in his hand. His hair has been shaved. His face is calm . . . amused, even. He is adored and he is despised. He is a hero and a villain. He is everything to everyone.*

CECILIA: The Lord is my shepherd; I shall not want. He maketh me to lie down in green pastures: he leadeth me beside the still waters. He restoreth my soul.

> *Hesitantly, MARIE-ANGELIQUE joins CECILIA and holds her hand.*

CECILIA & MARIE-ANGELIQUE: He leadeth me in the paths of righteousness for his name's sake. Yea, though I walk through the valley of the shadow of death, I will fear no—

LOUIS RIEL is hanged. EUGENIA grabs their hands but does not join in the prayer.

. . . evil: for thou art with me; thy rod and thy staff they comfort me.

His body twitches.

Thou preparest a table before me in the presence of mine enemies . . .

The rope creaks and groans.

Thou anointest my head with oil.

It sways back and forth.

My cup runneth over.

And back and forth.

Surely goodness and mercy shall follow me all the days of my life.

And back and forth . . .

And I will dwell in the house of the Lord . . .

. . . until coming to a gentle stop.

. . . forever.

Some time passes.

EUGENIA: The people were crying.

MARIE-ANGELIQUE: The sun was shining.

CECILIA: The frost made everything glitter, like diamonds.

MARIE-ANGELIQUE: I love diamonds.

EUGENIA: Last words:

LOUIS RIEL: Mr. John A. Macdonald, I send you a message. I have not the honour to know you personally . . . Do not let yourself be completely carried away by the glories of power.

CECILIA: They say his face looked calm before they covered it with the white cap.

EUGENIA: They say he held a silver crucifix in his hand and kissed it.

MARIE-ANGELIQUE: Some called him a traitor.

CECILIA: Some say he was a hero.

EUGENIA: No matter what history calls him, he shall never be forgotten.

MARIE-ANGELIQUE: Not like us. I wish . . . I wish I could be remembered, too. I don't want to be forgotten.

EUGENIA: Me neither.

CECILIA: Me neither.

A long, sad pause.

MARIE-ANGELIQUE: What shall we do now?

CECILIA: We keep fighting.

MARIE-ANGELIQUE: But I'm so tired.

CECILIA: Then first we shall rest.

MARIE-ANGELIQUE: But there's no time.

EUGENIA: There's all the time in the world. Come on. Let's have some tea and put on some furs.

CECILIA: I love tea.

MARIE-ANGELIQUE: I love furs.

> *The women rock back and forth and back and forth and back and forth. The water boils. The baby cries. The gunshots blare. The horses gallop. There are too many sounds.*

"I know that through the grace of God, / I am the founder of Manitoba."

CECILIA: "We must cherish our inheritance. We must preserve / our nationality for the youth of our future. The story should be written down to pass on."

> *CECILIA begins to cough.*

EUGENIA: "Deeds are not accomplished in a few days, or in a few hours. / A century is only a spoke in the wheel of everlasting time."

MARIE-ANGELIQUE: "I am more convinced every day that without a single exception I did right. And I have always believed that, as I have acted / honestly, the time will come when the people of Canada will see and acknowledge it."

CECILIA: "I have nothing but my heart and I have given it long ago to my country."

> *CECILIA stops coughing and falls asleep.*

EUGENIA: "In a little while it will be over. We may fail. But the rights / for which we contend will not die."

EUGENIA falls asleep.

MARIE-ANGELIQUE: "My people will sleep for one hundred years, but when they awake, it will be the artists who give them their spirit back."

MARIE-ANGELIQUE falls asleep.

The women sleep for one hundred years.

Then they wake up.

The end.

STUDY GUIDE

BY ASHLEY WILLIAMSON

This tool will help teachers and students analyze Women of the Fur Trade *by Frances Koncan. It includes historical context and discussion prompts to use before, during, and after reading the play. For those who may not have read a play before, suggestions for how to approach reading a play are also included.*

HOW TO READ A PLAY

Before You Read: What do you already know about this play? How does it fit in with other things you are reading or have read for class?

While You Read: Identify and define any unfamiliar terms. Use a dictionary. *The Canadian Oxford Dictionary* is a good resource.

Put down your highlighter! Make marginal notes or comments using a pencil instead. Every time you feel the urge to highlight something, write instead. Ask questions, offer interpretations, track characters or themes.

Make a diagram or family tree of characters and their relationships to one another.

Keep track of what happens on stage versus what happens off stage— what we are shown versus what we are told.

Read the play out loud, preferably with other people. Plays come to life when seen and heard.

Find photographs or a video of this play online so you can visualize the action you're reading about. Make note of what is different between the script and the production, or notes about the acting, costumes, or set choices.

After You Read: Summarize what you have read and learned. Pretend you are explaining it to a friend from class, if that helps. Or record yourself talking about it. Organizing your thoughts about what you have read can clarify things that weren't immediately obvious to you.

HISTORICAL CONTEXT: TERMS, PEOPLE, AND PLACES

This section fills out the historical landscape of the play by offering a primer on the period before and immediately after Confederation. It is by no means a comprehensive account of events, people, and places but rather a foundation for further study.

Timeline of Events Relevant to the Métis Resistance 1869–1885

Pre-colonization | The Forks, the site where the Red and Assiniboine Rivers join, is maintained as an important meeting place for Indigenous peoples for at least 6,000 years. The Forks and the area of what is now known as southern Manitoba is the home and traditional lands of the Anishinaabe, Ininew, and Dakota peoples.

1811 | The Red River Colony is established by Thomas Douglas, the Earl of Selkirk, on a 300,000 square kilometre land grant that covers most of southern Manitoba.

1821 | A merger of the North West Company and the Hudson's Bay Company boosts immigration of Scottish and French Métis families to the Red River Colony.

1846 | Led by Alexander "Koonaubay" Isbister, the Métis people petition the British government to be acknowledged as a distinct culture, with the Red River Colony granted status as a recognized British colony.

1867 | Canadian Confederation: three British colonies—the Province of Canada (which will split to become Ontario and Quebec), Nova Scotia, and New Brunswick—unite to form the Dominion of Canada.

1869 | The Hudson's Bay Company sells its rights to Rupert's Land— which included the whole of Manitoba (including the Red River Colony), most of Saskatchewan, southern Alberta, southern Nunavut, and the northern portions of Ontario and Quebec—to the Dominion of Canada.

October–November 1869 | Threatened by a survey party sent to the Red River Colony by the Canadian government and the negotiation of the land transfer without their involvement, the Métis—under separate groups led by Louis Riel and William Dease—form the Métis National Committee to represent Métis interests and to call for the formation of a Métis nation. The committee occupies Upper Fort Garry in what is now Winnipeg and turn back the survey party.

8 December 1869 | The Métis form a provisional government with Louis Riel as leader and begin negotiations with the Dominion government for Rupert's Land to formally enter Canadian Confederation.

March 1870 | Irish Protestant settler Thomas Scott is executed at Fort Garry. Riel's level of involvement in the execution is unclear, but Scott's death strains relations between the Métis and the Canadian federal government.

April 1870 | The Métis and the Canadian government negotiate in Ottawa for the Red River Colony to join confederation, with provisions from the Métis to include bilingual denominational schools, judicial and parliamentary systems, and measures to maintain their title to the land. Attempts to secure amnesty for Riel fail.

12 May 1870 | The Manitoba Act is passed and the territory officially becomes a province. Métis land rights are recognized as part of the deal.

May–August 1870 | The Red River Expeditionary Force of 700 militiamen is created by the Canadian federal government and sent to Manitoba to ensure the peaceful transfer of power. Riel and his supporters are fearful that the expedition will act punitively towards those who formed the provisional government.

24 August 1870 | Riel and some supporters flee to the US.

1870–1885 | Led by the Canadian government under John A. Macdonald, and contrary to promises made under the Manitoba Act, land grabs and military settlement around Winnipeg, initiated by the Red River Expeditionary Force, drive the Manitoba Métis westward.

1872 | Saskatchewan Métis petition to form a colony of 1,800,000 acres.

Summer 1884 | The Métis of Saskatchewan convince Louis Riel to return to Canada to petition the federal government on their behalf.

18 March 1885 | The Provisional Government of Saskatchewan is established with Louis Riel as president and Gabriel Dumont as adjutant general, declaring independence from the Dominion of Canada.

26 March 1885 | The Battle of Duck Lake marks the beginning of the North-West Resistance.

9 May 1885 | At the Battle of Batoche, Métis groups effectively resist Canadian forces for three days but are ultimately defeated.

20 July–1 August 1885 | Louis Riel is tried and found guilty of high treason by Crown prosecutors.

16 November 1885 | Louis Riel is executed for treason in Regina.

A Short Summary of the Red River Resistance

The Red River Resistance of 1869–1870 was an uprising of local residents against the transfer of Rupert's Land from the Hudson's Bay Company to the new Dominion of Canada. The participants in the resistance were mostly Métis hunters and farmers, the descendants of French-speaking *voyageur* and *coureurs des bois*, early Scottish settlers, and nehiyaw and Ojibwe buffalo hunters.

The Red River Colony was founded in 1811 by Lord Selkirk at the confluence of the Red and Assiniboine Rivers, in what is now called Winnipeg. The two main fur trading posts of the region were the North West Company's Fort Gibraltar and a small Hudson's Bay Company outpost in what is now St. Boniface. In 1836, the Hudson's Bay Company (HBC) added this settlement to its already massive holdings in Rupert's Land, but as Canada moved towards Confederation and the American government moved to settle the west, the HBC decided that selling off their land holdings to the Dominion of Canada would be more cost-effective than keeping them.

Trading and land control had never been easy for the Métis residents of Red River while the HBC was managing the area, but the Métis feared that a transfer to Canadian authority posed a threat to their language and culture. While the Métis negotiated with Canada over the transfer of power, English-speaking Protestant settlers from the east were moving into the colony and creating conflict. Given that the Canadian government was itself largely anglophone and Protestant, anxiety abounded that the Métis—who were a majority French Catholic—might lose everything.

Early sources of tension included efforts by Canadian surveyors to redraw property lines. The settlement had been organized in the French seignorial manner of long rectangular lots so that each farm had access to the river. The English, however, favoured square lots that cut many parcels of land off from the water and community. Many Métis did not have a clear title to their land, and although Ottawa said it would respect occupancy rights, its promise was not kept. When William McDougall, an anglophone Canadian expansionist, was appointed lieutenant-governor of the territory, the trust broke down further.

It was at this critical juncture that Louis Riel became the spokesperson for the Métis. Riel and his resistors, a group that initially included both anglophones and francophones, held off the land surveyors and prevented the transfer of control to the Canadian government on 1 December 1869. The resistance seized control of Upper Fort Garry and held it until the government agreed to negotiate. A provisional government was formed with Louis Riel as its leader and talks began to bring the territory into Confederation.

The armed conflict at Upper Fort Garry continued into the winter and spring of 1870, with Riel maintaining control until he agreed to execute Thomas Scott, an English-speaking settler from Ontario. The execution cemented distrust and fury amidst the federal government, anglophones, and eastern Canadians toward Riel and his followers. Many Métis felt that Scott's execution undermined their position. Negotiations with the Canadian government continued but Riel was denied amnesty as part of their diplomacy and he eventually fled the country, fearing prosecution. This chain of events inspired the popular perception of Louis Riel as a traitor and a villain, an attitude that persisted for generations.

On 12 May 1870, the province of Manitoba joined the Canadian Confederation. The Canadian government assured the people of Red River that their land titles would be honoured and that 607,000 hectares of land would be held for their children. These promises were poorly enforced, when they were enforced at all, and what little confidence the people of Red River still had in the new Manitoba government diminished even further. Many from the settlement moved west.

Riel spent the intervening years in Quebec and various parts of the us, eventually ending up in Montana where he married, had children, and worked as a school teacher. In 1884 he was persuaded to return to Canada to help the Métis of what would become Saskatchewan resist the Canadian government survey and reallotment of their land. Many of the Saskatchewan Métis had moved west from the Red River Colony after the creation of Manitoba, and they were dismayed to experience the same old problems in their new home.

Riel's return marked the start of the five-month North-West Resistance, which started with the Battle of Duck Lake and the retreat of the North-West Mounted Police and ended with the three-day Battle of Batoche that effectively put an end to the resistance. Riel surrendered to the Canadian militia and was tried and executed in Regina in April 1885.

Names and Terms

Coureurs des bois were unlicensed fur traders. They were known as "wood-runners" in English and "bush-lopers" to the Anglo-Dutch. Unlike *voyageurs, coureurs des bois* did not have permits from colonial authorities to engage in trade.

Gabriel Dumont (December 1837–19 May 1906) was a Métis leader and ally of Louis Riel who played a key role in the 1885 North-West Resistance. Dumont was born at the Red River Settlement and died in Bellevue, Saskatchewan.

Fort Garry was a Hudson's Bay Company trading post located at the junction of the Assiniboine and Red Rivers in what is now central Winnipeg, Manitoba.

The Hudson's Bay Company (HBC) was given its charter on 2 May 1670, making it the oldest merchandizing company in the English-speaking world. HBC was a fur-trading business for most of its history and played a significant role in the colonization of British North America and the creation of Canada.

John A. Macdonald (10 or 11 January 1815–6 June 1891) was the first prime minister of Canada. He was in office from 1867–1873 and then again from 1878–1891 and was the key figure within the Dominion government during the Red River and North-West Resistances. He was born in Glasgow, Scotland, and died in Ottawa.

William McDougall (25 January 1822–29 May 1905) was the expansionist lieutenant-governor of Rupert's Land and the North-Western Territory (the territories that would become Manitoba, Saskatchewan, and parts of Alberta) who espoused deep anti-Catholic and anti-Indigenous views. He was born in York, Upper Canada, and died in Ottawa, Ontario.

Métis are people of mixed European and Indigenous ancestry and one of the three recognized Indigenous peoples of Canada.

The North West Company (NWC) was founded in 1779 and was part of the fur trade from the 1780s to 1821. The NWC was managed by Scottish immigrants living in Montreal and Empire Loyalists who came north to escape the American Revolution. The company relied on French Canadian labour.

The Red River Colony was a settlement at the Forks, where the Red and Assiniboine Rivers joined, and whose boundaries crossed parts of what are now Manitoba and North Dakota.

Louis Riel (22 October 1844–16 November 1885) was a Métis leader, an important figure in the Red River and North-West Resistances, and is considered the founder of Manitoba. Riel was born in St. Boniface, Red River Colony, and died in Regina, North-West Territories.

Rupert's Land was a far-reaching territory of northern wilderness that the Hudson's Bay Company effectively controlled from 1670 to 1870. Named for Prince Rupert, the HBC's first governor, it was primarily a trapping ground for the fur trade. In 1869 the Government of Canada acquired Rupert's Land, which encompassed roughly a third of what is now Canada, from the HBC. Rupert's Land eventually became parts of Quebec, Ontario, Manitoba, Saskatchewan, Alberta, and Nunavut.

Thomas Scott (1 January 1842–4 March 1870) was an Irish Protestant born in Clandeboye, County Down, Ireland, and moved to the Red River Colony in 1869, joining the Canadian Party. Scott was convicted of treason and executed by the Métis National Committee's provisional government on 4 March 1870.

Voyageurs were 18th- and 19th-century French Canadian trappers who transported furs by canoe during the North American fur trade. Voyageurs were licensed to transport goods to forts and posts but were usually forbidden to do any trading of their own.

DISCUSSION QUESTIONS

History, Story, and Writing

The playwright inserts details that suggest her play isn't totally true, such as calling where the women live "the Reddish River" rather than the Red River. Can you find other examples of this in the text? What are some of the reasons why the playwright might want you to remember that you're reading fiction?

At the end of the play, Eugenia says that history is written by the victors. What does this mean to you? If this play is about the "losers," the people whose stories didn't get to be recorded, then is it still history, or is it something else?

Several characters in this play are shown reading, writing, or dictating letters. What do you think it's like to watch a play in which so much information comes from characters reciting or dictating letters?

Marie-Angelique's letters are dictated to Cecilia, who writes them out with neat handwriting; the replies that Marie-Angelique thinks are from Louis Riel are actually written by Thomas Scott. Does this diminish the authenticity of the letters' content? What do you make of the fact that it's the two white settler characters doing the writing on behalf of the two Métis characters?

Stage Space and Social Status

Why do you think the playwright has the women sitting in a particular order? How does it relate to their identity or status? What do you make of the fact that after Marie-Angelique is able to leave the room Eugenia takes her chair and moves it so close to Cecilia?

Who can leave the fort and who can't? Why do you think this is significant? Why do you think the women are always on stage, even when Louis Riel and Thomas Scott have scenes together in locations that are not the fort?

Visualize how you think the stage would look during a performance. How else might the play be using relationships in space to represent relationships between people or ideas?

Treason and Betrayal

Near the end of the play, the women call Louis Riel both a traitor and a hero; why would he be both?

The play depicts Riel and Scott as having a friendlier relationship than they might have had in real life. This makes Scott's death feel like it's a personal betrayal as well as an act of political violence. Why insert this personal betrayal into the story?

Who else in this play is a traitor, and who else suffers betrayal? How do the characters handle betrayal? Why do you think some characters react to betrayal differently than others do?

Comedy and Tragedy

Despite containing tragic situations, this play tells much of its story through comedy. What are some examples of scenes that seem designed to make you laugh at a serious situation? Why do you think the playwright would do that?

Language

The actions of Louis Riel and his Métis National Committee are most often labelled as a "resistance" at this time in history, but for many years they were called rebels and their actions labelled as rebellion. Using a good dictionary, look up the definition of "resistance" and "rebellion." What are the key differences between these words? Why would it be advantageous for the 1870 Canadian government to use one instead of the other? What about the Métis?

ACKNOWLEDGEMENTS

There are probably a lot of people I should acknowledge here, because that is the respectful thing to do. Days before writing this acknowledgement, I read that you should keep an ongoing list of all the people you need to acknowledge. I wish I had read that sooner. Alas, I kept no such list, and so I would like to take over this section and turn it into an apology section, where I humbly beg for forgiveness for all the people I have forgotten to acknowledge. Besties, your contributions were legit unforgettable.

Frances Koncan is a writer of mixed Anishinaabe and Slovene descent from Couchiching First Nation in Treaty 3 territory, and currently living and working on Treaty 1 territory in Winnipeg, Manitoba. She learned to write by fighting with adults on the Internet in the late '90s before Internet safety was a consideration. Their theatrical career began in 2007 when they saw a production of *The Threepenny Opera* starring Alan Cumming and he accidently touched her shoulder. In her free time, she likes playing video games and adding expensive luxury goods to her online shopping cart with no intention of ever checking out.